Learning
from the Past

Five Cases of
Aboriginal Justice

John Steckley

Library and Archives Canada Cataloguing in Publication

Steckley, John
    Learning from the past : five cases of Aboriginal justice

Includes bibliographical references and index.

ISBN 978-1-897160-77-0

de Sitter Publications
111 Bell Dr., Whitby, ON,
L1N 2T1, Canada

deSitterPublications.com
289-987-0656
info@desitterpublications.com

Contents

Introduction

Judge Murray Sinclair, an Aboriginal person of the Saulteaux people of Western Canada, wrote,

> in the 19th century, Canada...enacted laws depriving Aboriginal people of the right to contract, to sell property, to engage in business, to establish successful farms, to vote, to go to court, to raise their children, to practise their spiritual beliefs, to manage their own affairs, and to select their governments in accordance with their traditions. Canada had authorized its agents of authority, including the police, to arrest Aboriginal people without warrant simply for being outside the boundaries of their communities without written permission.[1] Aboriginal children had been removed from their homes and raised in oppressive and often racist residential school environments in which they were told it was "bad to be an Indian." (Sinclair as cited in Hamilton, 2001, p. 5)

John Alan Lee notes a misleading and harmful set of assumptions about Aboriginal people and the Canadian justice system made by a pair of Canadian sociologists:

> The efforts of the legal establishment to maintain the fiction that Canadian law is blind to race are aided...by the efforts of sociologists....Bienvenue and Latif (1975)[2] found that native/Indians were greatly overrepresented in 6,000 sentences in Winnipeg courts, but argue that no discrimination existed. They suggest that Indians land in jail proportionately more often than whites because Indians prefer to go to jail. They consider it "a shared experience, a chance to rest...get better food and meet old friends." Native Indians do not find this line of reasoning amusing. (Lee as cited in Grayson, 1983, pp. 515-516)

In a later chapter we will discuss the concept of blaming the victim, which this quotation exemplifies. Examples of the blame-the-victim phenomenon include blaming a rape on the clothes that a woman is wearing, and blaming a breed of dog by banning it, when it is the owners that are mostly at fault.

In discussing the case of Sinnisiak and Uluksuk, two Inuit suspects in a murder case, the *Calgary Herald* of August 11, 1917 printed the following unrealistic portrayal. The people being discussed were the Copper Inuit (an ethnicity within the Inuit) who probably numbered about 1,000 over a widespread area at the time, and who, at the most, would number 100 and 200 in the largest single gathering within a year. This journalist was talking about the peaceful apprehension of the two prisoners by the RCMP.

> [H]ere on the rim of the world were a people who knew not the law or the law bringers–by the slightest error the patrol would bring upon itself the fury of a thousand warriors–warriors who could send with their mighty arms the copper tip birch arrow through the body of a Caribou at a hundred paces. Warriors who knew no fear in battle. (Robin, 1976, p. 177)

The writer's description here betrays his ignorance of the Arctic and the Inuit. At that point, there probably had never been a time in history when 1,000 Inuit were together in one place. Battles of any size in Inuit history were few and far between. And caribou were usually shot from a short distance, as the Inuit were skilled hunters, more than able to sneak up on unsuspecting caribou. But that amount of truth wouldn't make the story sound so heroic.

This book is about five cases in which Canadian Aboriginal people have been abused by the Canadian justice system, a system of Aboriginal injustice: J. J. Harper, Helen Betty Osborne, Donald Marshall Jr., Minnie Sutherland, and Neil Stonechild. Each case has had a book written about it. Each book details a horror story, with little justice in sight for the near future. Almost every case has had an inquest, inquiry, or even a royal commission dedicated to identifying the wrong done, with suggestions for change.

What I am trying to do with this book is to take each case a few steps farther. The story will be told. Wrongs will be identified. Suggestions for change will be made, relating to what has happened since, good and bad. Added to each story will be similar stories that show that these cases are not isolated events. Readers are encouraged to think of what they would do to change the situation, as change is necessary.

The Purpose of this Chapter

Support for Aboriginal people in Canada is like soil in the Prairies–it is wide but not deep. While many, perhaps most, Canadians are supportive of Aboriginal causes when they arise in the popular media, as the Idle No More movement (arguably) illustrates, their understanding of the underlying causes is sadly shallow. The purpose of this introductory chapter is to present a short backgrounder to add a little depth to that understanding.

Aboriginal people have been in most parts of Canada for at least 12,000 years, a conservative figure. The ancestors from most Aboriginal people in the Americas may have arrived in these continents 15,000 years ago. For the first 11,000 years, about 550 generations, roughly 92% of the human history of this land, they were the only people in what is now Canada. This makes for a tremendous connection to this land, and a right to claim Aboriginal rights both morally and legally. Think of what your link to a family farm would be if it had been in family for five generations.

The document that first spoke strongly of those rights was the **Royal Proclamation of 1763**, (see Steckley and Cummins, 2008, pp. 121-122), which, along with settling things as much as possible between the British and the French after the British militarily defeated the French, discussed how Aboriginal land was to be acquired: through "public purchase," in other words **treaties** (see Steckley and Cummins, 2008, pp. 136-137). From the time of the Royal Proclamation to the first decades of the twentieth century, various treaties were signed. Not all Aboriginal peoples signed treaties (British Columbia is very confused in this regard), but most did. Each treaty was a little different from the others–vague in places, particularly when it came to Aboriginal rights; more concrete in others, particularly when it came to Aboriginal duties. By the 1780s, treaties typically involved a massive land transfer, with monies being promised, often held "in trust" by the governments involved, and with a smaller piece or pieces of land being "reserved" for the use of the Aboriginal group involved. That is why those pieces of land are called **reserves** (see Steckley and Cummins, 2008, p. 133). The United States uses the term "reservations" for similar pieces of land.

To understand better what treaties are, as they are thought of by Aboriginal people, it is necessary to quote an Aboriginal person, although not everyone thinks alike when it comes to these important documents. We must speak of Aboriginal views, rather than a single, homogeneous Aboriginal view.

The people can be divided in their opinions based on gender, class, urban versus rural residence, and so on. But there are distinct tendencies, as the following words from Nisga Chief Joesph Gosnell illustrate. Finally, at the beginning of the twenty-first century, after a century of arguing with the government, his people signed a treaty.

> To us, a treaty is a sacred instrument. It represents an understanding between distinct cultures and shows respect for each other's way of life. We know we are here for a long time together. A treaty stands as a symbol of high idealism in a divided world. (Gosnell as cited in Rose, 2000, p. 22)

Such a view is very common among many "treaty Indians."

A Diversity of Cultures, a Mono-cultural Plan?

Traditionally, a broad diversity of Aboriginal peoples has existed in this land. For example, there is no single "Indian" language (no matter how many times older English dictionaries refer to words borrowed into English as merely "Indian" in origin). There were and are still are 11 different language groups, with the diversity being expressed particularly in British Columbia. There are seven **language families** (groups of related languages): Algonquian, Athapaskan, Eskimo-Aleut, Iroquoian, Salish, Siouan, Salish, and Wakashan. Then there are **language isolates**, languages with no known relatives. There are four of them in Canada, including Kutenai,

Tsimshian, Haida, and Tlingit, all of which are spoken in British Columbia. The 11 groups all still have speakers, but within those groups, only 50 languages still have speakers, some with fewer than 100 individuals, most of them old, who can talk in their "Native" tongue. Government policy, especially educational policy through the residential schools, was directed against the speaking of these languages. This language oppression is common in **colonial** situations, including Austronesian speakers in Taiwan, Ainu speakers in Japan, and speakers of Aborigine languages in Australia. Punishment could be harsh, abuse not uncommon.

There was also a diversity of socio-political structures among various groups, from smaller nomadic[3] **bands** to more sedentary (i.e., live in one place year round) **tribes, chiefdoms**, and **confederacies**, to use some anthropological terms. Housing varied from elm bark and cedar pole "longhouses" in what is now Ontario and the massive log structures in British Columbia that, in a few cases, could hold as many as 100 people and stood for generations, to more temporary dwellings that could only hold a nuclear family as long as a site provided them with food. Here, the words "tipi" (Siouan), "wigwam" (Algonquian), and "igloo" (Inuktitut) come to mind.

A succession of Canadian federal governments carved up that political diversity into one-strategy-fits-all **bands**. **Tribes** (e.g., Haida, Chipewyan, Mohawk, and Mi'kmaq) no longer had an official corporate representation. They also shrunk the housing diversity by forcing people to live in European-model, outsider-designed, and often poorly conceived and constructed reserve housing. All communities became, by an act of Parliament, politically isolated bands to be governed by majority-rule elected chief and council, no matter what their traditional larger allegiances and forms of governance had been (which often involved **consensus** rather than majority rule). Whatever the original reasons for setting up these political structures (administrative simplicity, perhaps), it became an effective colonial mode of "divide and conquer," breaking down any form of social resistance, as did isolating people in far flung reserves.

While words such as colonialism and conquer are used here, and Canadian Aboriginal people tended to take sides with the French against the British and with the British against the Americans in a series of "white wars." Despite the occasional battles and raids, there were no sustained winner-take-all "Indian Wars" like those that took place intermittently in the United States from the 1600s to the early twentieth century. This is not to make Canada seem than much nicer than the United States; we just committed a more subtle form of oppression in this country: death by cold bureaucracy.

The Indian Act

The **Indian Act** was introduced to Canadian law by the federal government in 1876 (see Steckley and Cummins, 2008, pp. 122-123), after it had given itself the power to rule over Aboriginal people in 1867. The Indian Act gave a succession of governments tremendous control over band communities (see the following examples). Initially, responsibility for the Indian Act was given to the Department of Mines and Resources, then to Citizenship and Immigration (an ironic touch), and finally to Northern Affairs and National Resources, which is currently known as Aboriginal Affairs and Northern Development. Some older books refer to it as the Department of Indian Affairs (DIA) and the Department of Indian Affairs and Northern Development (DIAND), two purposes often set against each other.

Control Under the Indian Act

The Indian Act gives much of the legal justification for this high level of governance as the following two small examples illustrate. The Indian Act stipulates that soil cannot be transferred from the reserve to off of the reserve. In 2011, in the Musée-Huron-Wendat, a museum in Wendake, the sole remaining Huron community in Canada, there was a series of exhibits about the Indian Act. One was an interactive and creative art display that featured pictures of the artist digging up reserve soil and putting it into a bag. In front of these pictures were small bags of sand. The visitors were encouraged to share in her "crime" by taking one of those little bags before they leave the reserve. I use this exhibit in a sociology course that I teach to police foundation students. In the first class, I say to them, "I have in this bag a substance that is illegal in the way that I obtained it. What is it?" After their failed guesses (almost all of them related to drugs), I tell them what it is and explain to them that the socio-legal definition of this substance makes it sociologically different from all other sand in Canada.

Another exhibit at the museum was a picture of a boy with painted rocks. The Indian Act specifies that you cannot take painted rocks from a reserve. The exhibitor bought his son a set of paints and got him to paint several small reserve rocks. He then sent a letter to Indian Affairs asking whether it would be okay for his son to take the rocks off of the reserve. The return letter, part of the exhibit, was long, but it did not exactly say "no," and it did not exactly say "yes" either.

Three Main Legal and Ethnic Distinctions

There are three different kind of legal entities that are Aboriginal: **registered Indian** (the term used to be status Indian), **Métis**, and **Inuit**. The first are those people who the Indian Act deems as legally "Indian," and these people are the main subjects of this book.

Métis

As defined by the people themselves (or at least their organizational leaders), a Métis is "a person who self-identifies as Métis, is distinct from other Aboriginal peoples [i.e., registered Indians and Inuit], is of Historic Métis Nation ancestry, and is accepted by the Métis Nation" (www.albertametis.com). The three key elements they depend on for definition, then, are self-identification, genetic ancestry, and group acceptance by Métis.

The word Métis is based on a French word meaning "mixed." The initial mixture that gave birth to the Métis occurred between an Aboriginal group (usually the Cree, less often the Saulteaux) and a European one (usually the French, but also the Scots) with the western movement of the fur trade in the second half of the eighteenth century.

The homeland or territory that is typically part of this identity extends from northwest Ontario (i.e., Sault Ste.

Marie) to the eastern part of British Columbia. In the 2006 census, there were roughly 404,000 Métis.

The mixture was of more than just genes. The language they came to use was a unique blend of Cree (usually verbs) and French (usually nouns), known as **Michif**. The broader cultural mix they developed early involved the Catholic Church, agriculture, draft and riding animals, and guns, but employed hunting practices and knowledge of buffalo and the land compiled and honed through the centuries in Plains Cree culture.

The Métis developed a sense of nationhood through conflict with the controlling interests of the Hudson's Bay Company and the Dakota enemies of the Plains Cree. This conflict, plus the lack of governmental respect for the land rights and culture of the Métis, led to the resistance that is identified with the Métis leader Louis Riel (of French and Chipewyan ancestry) in 1869-70 and 1884-85, which are often referred to somewhat misleadingly as the "Riel Rebellions." The Métis ultimately lost those conflicts and have been fighting for rights and identity recognition ever since. In January 2013, the Supreme Court declared that the Métis were a federal responsibility, like Indians and Inuit, but, as I write (February 2013), this ruling is being appealed by the federal government, who are trying to get away from such responsibilities.

The Inuit

The ancestors of the Inuit[4] were the last Aboriginal group to travel from Asia to the Americas. Related groups still exist in Siberia. The term Inuit means "people." The singular is Inuk. There is no word, "Inuits." There are roughly 55,700 Inuit who live in 53 communities in Nunavut ("Our Land"), Labrador, Quebec, and the Northwest Territories. They have a legal status in Canada that is both shared, when it comes to Aboriginal rights, and distinct in terms of the Indian Act.

Although the Inuit could not be completely considered Canadian citizens until 1939, they were prosecuted under Canadian law before that time, as we'll see in the Sinnisiak and Uluksuk story. The definition of who is an Inuk has varied over the years. Beginning in 1941, they were issued discs (don't leave home without it) and held disc numbers that "proved" their legal identity. In the 1975 James Bay Agreement, someone living in Quebec would be considered an Inuk if he or she possessed a disc number, had one-quarter Inuit blood, or was considered to be an Inuk by an Inuit community (that is by history, genetics, or group recognition). Discs and disc numbers were used until 1978.

One of the negative aspects of the Inuit relationship between Inuit and federal governments since 1939 has involved the forced movement of whole communities (or individuals with tuberculosis),[5] with generally disastrous results. The best-known movement had the people of Inukjuak move some 3,200 kilometres north from Quebec by the eastern shores of Hudson Bay to Grise Fiord, Ellesmere Island. This move could help Canada claim that territory because they could then demonstrate that they had a community there. An official apology for that move came from the federal government on August 18, 2010 (see Zarate [2010] for a discussion of this apology).

Sinnisiak and Uluksuk[6]

Sinnisiak and Uluksuk were the first Inuit tried for murder under Canadian law. In 1911, the region the two men called home was still relatively unknown to non-Native people. Canada's legal status in the territory was based more on assumption than on concrete substance. The federal government did not assume legal responsibility for the welfare of Inuit in the Arctic (as they had for all other Canadians) until compelled to do so by a 1939 decision of the Supreme Court.

In July 1911, Father Jean-Baptiste Rouviere arrived at Fort Norman, at the junction of the Bear and Mackenzie Rivers, the leaping off point to the barren lands of the extreme North. He spent some time with the people until they moved north in October. The next spring, he was joined by another missionary, Father Guillaume Le Roux, who, like him, was a native of France. Unlike Rouviere, who seems to have been fairly easy going, Le Roux appears to have lacked patience and self-control. He was said to be aggressive, overbearing, and prone to fits of rage.

In the summer and early fall of 1912, the two Catholic missionaries met with the Inuit. It is not known what the Inuit thought of the priests early on, whether they were clear on how the missionaries differed from the other white men, the traders, who visited them. Material goods were offered to any Inuit who would spend the winter at Fort Norman. The Inuit did not see that as practical for their hunting and general survival needs, so they refused to come and stay.

The next year, Rouviere and Le Roux decided to travel north in the winter. The two men lacked the skills and knowledge necessary to function effectively in the Arctic, so the Inuit had to take care of them. One man, Kormik, hunted for Le Roux, while Uluksuk's wife made the priests winter clothes. To try to ensure cooperation, the missionaries distributed typical trade items such as needles, nets, and traps to the Inuit. Rifles were promised but were not forthcoming.

The two white men left for further north, the mouth of the Coppermine River, with Kormik and a number of others, including two young hunters named Sinnisiak and Uluksuk. All was not well. Some of the Inuit were growing disenchanted with the priests, who were a burden as they did not cope well with the hard travel. In addition, they saw the two white men as hoarding goods, not engaging with their culture norm of sharing. In addition, Le Roux was bellicose and belligerent, which, from an Inuit perspective, threatened the security of the group. When Kormik took a rifle in what he felt was payment for all the work he had done for the two men, Le Roux threatened him with a loaded gun.

The priests were unsure at this point as to what they should do. Within a few days of their arrival at the winter camp, they made the decision to return home.

They faced great difficulties as they travelled alone. They were inexperienced in facing the Arctic winter without Inuit assistance. They were tired from all the travelling. They had little food. Without the help from the Inuit whom they had just abandoned, they would die on the trail. On their second day out, they spotted Sinnisiak and Uluksuk returning to the winter camp. The priests convinced the two men to help them, telling them they would be paid with traps. The priests joined Sinnisiak and Uluksuk to the dogs in harness and forced them to pull the heavy sled until nightfall. The next morning, exhausted, and figuring that they had helped enough, the two

Inuit prepared to leave. They left only to be brought back by threats uttered by a rifle-bearing Le Roux. The Inuit would later testify that they asked Le Roux whether he would kill them if they didn't help, and the priest said that he would. The Inuit were put back in the harness with the dogs, and they set out in the middle of a blizzard. When they attempted to speak to the white men, the missionaries would cover the Inuit's mouths. Every time they slowed down or stopped, the priests pushed or threatened them with the rifle.

Eventually, Sinnisiak conveyed to Uluksuk the idea that he intended to kill their captors before the white men killed them. On the pretence of needing to relieve himself, Sinnisiak slipped out of his harness. When Le Roux relented and turned his back, Sinnisiak pounced on the man and stabbed him with a knife. The priest made a dash for the rifle on the sled, while Sinnisiak held Rouviere at bay with the bloody knife. Uluksuk and Le Roux fought for the rifle until the white man, stabbed several times, finally fell down dead. Rouviere ran for his life until he was brought down by a shot from Sinnisiak.

When the all-white jury gave their verdict it was "guilty of murder, with the strongest recommendation possible to mercy that the Jury can give" (Moyles, 1989, p. 8). In August 1917 the judge sentenced them to death by hanging. The death sentence was commuted by the governor general to life imprisonment. They served two years and were released. The RCMP termed them "model prisoners." The two Inuit men had helped the Mounties established a new post.

Residential Schools

No book about Aboriginal people and injustice would be complete without some reference to **residential schools**. These schools, most of which were initiated late in the nineteenth century, were (under)funded by the federal government and run by religious groups, including Catholic, Anglican, Presbyterian, and Methodist organizations. Aboriginal children were taken from their families and communities, often by the RCMP, and were housed in stern-looking buildings a long way from home (and of being home). These were not good schools in so many senses. With their being underfunded, not a lot of money was spent on teachers or teaching material. Students would sometimes spend a significant part of their school day being unpaid workers in farms run by the school. Costs were cut in terms of the food, sleeping room, and heat provided for the students. The children were crowded together and often undernourished. This made the schools easy places for tuberculosis to spread. The number of deaths came from those since the opening of the schools within the previous 20 years prior to the 1905-6 school year (Bryce, 1907).

And then there was the abuse. The children were physically, sexually, emotionally, and culturally abused. Cultural abuse involved a constant criticism of the culture that formed a major part of the children's identity and personal esteem. The chain of abuse that began with the residential school continued into Aboriginal communities. All studies show that a very high percentage of physical and sexual abusers were themselves abused once. At least three generations of Aboriginal people went to residential schools, some of which remained open until the 1980s. In 2006, it was reckoned that there were about 80,000 people still alive who had attended a residential school (Indian Residential School Resolution Canada, 2006). Sexual and physical abuse have both been identified as major social problems on a good number of reserves. Since 2006, the Truth and Reconciliation Commission has been in existence, trying to work out ways of financial compensation and healing to make up for the damage done to Aboriginal people. The healing process is far from over.

Racialization or Racializing

Sociologists and other social scientists today generally agree that it is more meaningful to speak of racialization or **racializing** as a process than of **race** as something biologically fixed or static. Racializing typically refers to categorizing groups of people in a hierarchical fashion, some being more positively valued or higher ranked, and others being more negatively valued or lower ranked. Aboriginal people are a racialized group in Canada, one that is generally negatively valued. We will be discussing the racializing of a number of different areas of life in this book: space, witnesses, and usual suspects. Take witnesses for example. In each of the cases discussed in this book, Aboriginal witnesses are automatically treated as unreliable, or at least as biased observers, the tools of justice act towards them as if they were (and they might be) considered suspects just by being Aboriginal. Non-Aboriginal witnesses are not treated this way. They seem to be thought of as neutral observers, with no particular bias. This dynamic also applies to potential jury members. An Aboriginal juror will be considered pro-Aboriginal, automatically, while a non-Aboriginal juror in an Aboriginal case is thought of as less likely to let his or her racialized status interfere with "justice."

Institutional or Systemic Racism

Probably the most important concept for readers to learn about in this book is that of **institutional(ized)** or **systemic racism**. This is racism that is part of the system or institutions of society. It appears in many places in a given society, discriminating against racialized groups in many ways, in laws, textbooks, media, and in the typical practices and behaviours of an organization. It perpetuates or reproduces itself readily and often exists, not at the conscious level, but just in unthinkingly doing things "as they have always been done." Stanley R. Barrett's words are key to the purpose of writing this book: "Effort is not required to maintain it [institutional racism]; instead, effort is required to diminish it" (Barrett, 1987, p. 308). The main reason for writing this book is to make an effort to do a little diminishing of the institutional or systemic racism with respect to the policing of Aboriginal people in Canada.

And while we are talking about racism, here is an important question. Can an Aboriginal person be racist? There are three components to racism, or at least to institutional racism. There is **prejudice**, which is a conscious attitude involving the "pre-judging" of someone because of their membership in a particular racialized group. Certainly, an Aboriginal person can have such an attitude towards non-Aboriginal people. Then there is **discrimination**, which typically involves applying prejudice. Discrimination can be defined as "acts by which individuals are differently rewarded or punished based on their membership in a social group defined by class, sexual orientation, ethnicity and so on" (Steckley & Letts, 2010, p. 410). Aboriginal people can discriminate, although they have relatively limited opportunities to do so, as they have limited power. Native studies departments can discriminate against non-Aboriginal scholars applying for jobs. The third component, which is hinted at by the last two sentences, is **power**. In this context, power refers to the conscious or unconscious ability to control situations in which discrimination can happen. Prejudice can be well hidden in institutional policies. In this sense, an Aboriginal people cannot be racist. They do not possess sufficient power.

Political Racism: The Vote

Canada became a country rather than a colony in 1867. The vote began with a very narrow focus. Only white men with property could vote federally or provincially. Part of a country being democratic entails a broad electorate, or group of people who vote. In the 146 years in which Canada has been a country (1867-2013), Aboriginal people have had the vote in all jurisdictions—federal, provincial, and territorial—for only 49 years, or a little over one third of that history. The following timeline sketches the legal impediments and milestones regarding enfranchisement in Canada:

1885   "Indians" west of Ontario are denied the vote; "Indian" males in and east of Ontario are given the vote only if they own land separate from the reserve and have made at least $150 worth of improvements. This involved very few people.

1898   "Indian" males east of Manitoba denied the federal vote regardless of property. White males without property were given the vote federally and provincially.

1949   "Indians" get the provincial vote in British Columbia and Newfoundland.

1952   "Indians" get the provincial vote in Manitoba.

1954   "Indians" get the provincial vote in Ontario.

1960	"Indians" get the federal vote, and also get the provincial and territorial vote in Yukon, Northwest Territories, and Saskatchewan.
1963	"Indians" get the provincial vote in New Brunswick and Nova Scotia.
1965	"Indians" get the provincial vote in Alberta.
1969	"Indians" get the provincial vote in Quebec.

A Racist Law:
Banning the Potlatch, Outlawing Religion

Laws make up a significant part of institutional or systemic racism. One of the best illustrations in Canadian history of a racist law is the Potlatch law, which is, strictly speaking, part of the Indian Act. Freedom of religion, like a broad electorate, is one of the basic components of a truly democratic country. In that sense, from 1884 to 1951, Canada could not be considered a truly democratic country, or one relatively free from systemic racism: religion was racialized. Here is the law as it was written:

> Every Indian or other person who engages in or assists in celebrating the Indian festival known as the "Potlatch"…is guilty of a misdemeanour, and shall be liable to imprisonment for a term of not more than six nor less than two months in any gaol or other place of confinement, and any Indian or other person who encourages, either directly or indirectly, an Indian or Indians to get up such a festival or dance, or to celebrate the same, or who shall assist in the celebration of same, is guilty of a like offence, and shall be liable to the same punishment. (Cited in Cummins & Steckley, 2003, p. 30)

This was, in some senses, a stricter law than were some of the drug laws of the day. The practices of the potlatch did not contain or encourage any illegal acts such as violence or the encouragement of violence. Alcohol or drugs were not involved. Names were validated. Many gifts were given. Music, dancing, acting, and storytelling took place. The biggest "potlatch bust" on record took place in 1921 when 45 of the most respected people of the Kwakiutl of Vancouver Island were arrested. Twenty-three were released, while 22 were sentenced to prison terms of two to three months.

Summary

In this brief introductory chapter, I have tried to supply a short backgrounder for the chapters that follow, making readers acquainted with some basic ideas necessary for understanding those chapters. As stated above, the first and foremost of those ideas is that of institutional or systemic racism. The cases discussed in the next five chapters all clearly demonstrate the effects of systemic racism.

Questions

1. What is misleading about the expression "is an Indian word for"?
2. How do you think the Sinnisiak and Uluksuk case should have been handled?
3. How valid is the statement "ignorance of the law is no excuse" in the Sinnisiak and Uluksuk case? Remember that Inuit culture had its own laws. People did not kill each other freely. No society allows for that.
4. Should there have been Inuit on the jury? How could that be arranged?
5. Why can institutional or systemic racism only be meaningfully practised by the dominant culture, not a minority culture?
6. What is meant by the statement that religion was racialized with the Potlatch law?
7. Why do you think that Aboriginal people were denied the vote for so long in Canada?

Key Terms

Aboriginal Affairs and Northern Development–the federal governmental body that exercises a significant amount of control over Aboriginal people in Canada.

band–a federally instituted group of registered Indians who have an elected chief and council, and special rights over reserve land. There is another meaning of the word "band." When anthropologists use the word, they are referring to small groups of people within a typically nomadic tribe who are in each other's presence for most or all of the year.

chiefdom–a distinct group of people who share a language, distinct culture, and differ from a tribe in having leaders with significant socio-political power.

colonial–a situation in which, typically, one group moves into the territory of another, dominates them, and devalues and oppresses their culture.

confederacy–a linked grouping of tribes who act together in large scale political situations (e.g., warfare). In Canada, this includes the Blackfoot Confederacy (including the Siksika or Blackfoot, Peigan, and Kainai or Blood) and the Haudenosaunee or Iroquois Confederacy (including the Seneca, Cayuga, Onondaga, Oneida, Mohawk, and Tuscarora).

consensus–involves everyone agreeing to a particular plan of action.

discrimination–the act of choosing in favour or against a member of a particular group based largely on their identifiable membership in that group.

Indian Act–the federal legislation that exercises a great deal of control over registered Indians in Canada. It originated in 1876 and has been altered several times, most notably 1951.

Inuit (singular **Inuk**)–"people"; a group of Aboriginal people who live in the Canadian north, and have an identity and genetic heritage separate from those of registered Indians and Métis.

Métis–a "mixed" (usually Cree-French) group of Aboriginal-European people in Canada who have a distinct history and identity separate from registered Indians and the Inuit.

Michif–a language formed primarily of a blending of Cree and French.

power–in sociological terms this relates to the ability to make others do what you want them to do.

prejudice–an attitude in which a member of a group is "pre-judged," usually in a negative way.

race–a group thought of as biologically different from other members of a species.

racializing or racialization–the social process through which certain groups are interpreted as being physically and socially different from other groups within a species.

registered Indian–someone who is "legally an Indian" in terms of the Indian Act.

reserves–lands reserved for people belonging to a particular band.

residential schools–boarding schools run for Aboriginal children by religions groups but paid for by the federal government.

Royal Proclamation of 1763–the legal basis from which the federal practice of signing treaties with Aboriginal people initiated.

treaties–document signed both by agents of the federal government and representatives of Aboriginal groups. Typically, treaties involved land transfer, a statement of rights and respect, monies that may or may not be fully transferred to the people, and promises that can be quite difficult to get federal governments to respect.

tribes–groups of people who typically speak one language, have one distinct culture, and usually shares a leadership that does not dominate or "order around" their people (e.g., Mi'kmaq, Chipewyan, and Delaware).

Notes

[1]   This is a reference to the pass laws, in which Aboriginal people living on prairie reserves had to obtain a pass from the Indian Agent, Farm Instructor of some other white person representing the federal government before they could leave their reserves (see Steckley & Cummins, 2001, pp. 218-219), a law that was in place from 1885 until the 1930s.

2   The source that Lee refers to here is actually, Bienvenue, P. & Latif, A.H. (1974). Arrests, Dispositions and Recidivism: A Comparison of Indians and Whites. *Canadian Journal of Criminology and Corrections, 16,* 105-116.

3   It should be pointed out that "nomadic" does not mean just wandering around, but entails going to specific places at different times of the year where resources are known to be. Nomadism as a lifestyle expresses extreme knowledge of the environment, not lack of purpose or plan.

4   The old word "Eskimo" comes from an Algonquian term for "eating something raw" (e.g., animal fat or blubber). It is related to the English terms "husky" and "squash." Using "Eskimo" is rather like calling the French "frog-eaters" or "frogs" or the Germans "sausage eaters."

5   During the 1950s, the Inuit had the highest tuberculosis rate in the world. The federal government did not respond by constructing small buildings in the north that could be used for the isolation and rest cure necessary for tuberculosis, as they did elsewhere earlier that century for other people. Instead, they sent a ship carrying x-ray machines for detecting tuberculosis. Those found with tuberculosis were quickly separated from families and friends and taken to southern Canada. From an Inuit perspective, many of their number dropped from sight and sound, buried but not forgotten (see Grygier, 1994).

6   This section is adapted from Cummins and Steckley (2003, pp. 146-149).

References

Barrett, S.R. (1987). *Is God a racist?* Toronto, ON: University of Toronto Press.

Bryce, P.H. (1907). *Report on the Indian schools of Manitoba and the North West Territory.* Ottawa, ON: Department of Indian Affairs.

Cummins, B.D., & Steckley, J.L. (2003). *Aboriginal policing: A Canadian perspective.* Toronto, ON: Pearson Canada.

Grayson, J.P. (1983). *Introduction to sociology: An alternate approach,* Toronto, ON: Gage Publishing Ltd.

Grygier, P. (1994.) *A long way from home: The tuberculosis epidemic among the Inuit.* Montreal, QC: McGill-Queen's University Press.

Hamilton, A.C. (2001). *A feather not a gavel: Working towards Aboriginal justice*. Winnipeg, MB: Great Plains Publications.

Moyles, R.G. (1989). *British law and Arctic men: The celebrated 1917 murder trials of Sinnisiak and Uluksuk, first Inuit tried under white man's law*. Burnaby, BC: Simon Fraser University.

Robin, M. (1976). *The bad and the lonely: Seven stories of the best-and worst-Canadian outlaws*. Toronto, ON: James Lorimer & Company.

Rose, A. (2000). *Spirit dance at Meziadin: Chief Joseph Gosnell and the Nisga'a Treaty*. Madeira Park, BC: Harbour Publishing.

Steckley, J.L., & Cummins, B.D. (2008). *Full circle: Canada's First Nations*. Toronto, ON: Pearson Canada.

Steckley, J.L., & Letts, G.K. (2010). *Elements of sociology: A critical Canadian introduction* (2nd ed.). Toronto, ON: Oxford University Press.

Zarate, G. (2010, September 11). For Grise Fiord's exiles an apology that came too late. *Nunatsiaq Online*. Retrieved from http:// www.nunatsiaqonline.ca

Chapter 1

The J.J. Harper Case

In an article that appeared in *Saturday Night* magazine, Constable Robert Cross of the Winnipeg Police Service (WPS) was quoted as saying the following:

> Harper was the author of his own demise. The natives drink and get into trouble. Blaming the police for their troubles is like an alcoholic blaming the liquor store for being open late. (Gillmor, 1988, p. 50)

In summing up their appraisal of the handling of the J.J. Harper case, the commissioners involved with the Manitoba Aboriginal Justice Inquiry explained,

> It is our conclusion that the City of Winnipeg Police Department did not search actively or aggressively for the truth about the death of J.J. Harper. Their investigation was, at best, inadequate. At worst, its primary objective seems to have been to exonerate Const. Robert Cross and to vindicate the Police Department. (www.majic.mb.ca)

Introduction

We begin our discussion of Aboriginal cases of injustice with the story of J.J. Harper. John Joseph Harper was many things. To use the terminology of sociology, he had many **statuses**, socially recognized positions in a society that have a relatively stable set of expectations regarding behaviour and attitude. J.J. Harper was a father, husband, Canadian citizen, Manitoban, executive director of the Island Lake Tribal Council, co-manager of a construction company, Cree, and

"Indian." When he came to the last day in his life, the last-named status trumped all the others. To the officer responsible for his death, "Indian" was the only one of Harper's statuses that he could see. In sociological terms, it was Harper's **master status**, the one that has the strongest impact on a person's identity. Police officers are social observers, in part by training, in larger part by personal experience. Nothing in this police officer's experience led him to see anything more than J.J. Harper's master status. Another sociological term is useful here: **status inconsistency**. Status consistency occurs when one's social status hierarchies line up; you are white, male, heterosexual, physically able, English-speaking, upper class with a powerful, well-paying job. Everything lines up. Each status is highly respected. When statuses do not align, when you earn good money (about $68,000, in Harper's case, which in 1988 was well above the Canadian average), are a respected political leader but you are Aboriginal, the condition is called status inconsistency. And often with status inconsistency, the lowest status rules, because the dominant society works that way. But learning to read people, such as is necessary in the policing and justice business, also means learning to pick up signs of all the statuses, not just the lowest-ranked one.

The Numbers Game behind the Story
Percentages

Manitoba has the highest percentage of Aboriginal people of any province in Canada. In 1986, the Aboriginal population was estimated at 93,450, 8.7% of the province's population. This was an underestimation, in part because a number of bands and individuals boycotted the census.[1] By 2001, this number had risen to 150,040, or about 13.6% of the population (Aboriginal People in Manitoba [APM], 2006, p.7). Manitoba also has the highest percentage of urban Aboriginal people of every province, with Winnipeg making up the bulk of that percentage. In 1951, there were reportedly only 210 Aboriginal people living in Winnipeg (Comack, 2012, p. 80), a city that then numbered about 354,000. From the 1950s to the 1990s, Aboriginal migration to the city was substantial. This migration presented a new challenge not only to the migrants but to municipal services, including the Winnipeg Police Service. In 1988, Winnipeg had a population of more than 660,000 people. In 1988, between 40,000 and 50,000 Aboriginals lived in the city of Winnipeg comprising between 6.0 and 7.5% of the city's population. (Frideres, 1998, p. 241). The 1,140-member police force had nine Native constables at that time, which represents about 0.8% of the force—less than one percent. In 2001, the official statistics had Aboriginals numbered at 51,720 within the municipal boundaries of Winnipeg, and 55,755 within the Census Metropolitan Area (APM, 2006, 16). Aboriginal urban statistics are notoriously difficult to calculate, in part because of the high mobility of their population.

Two opposing key concepts are important here: **under-representation** and **over-representation**. Aboriginal people were under-represented in the Winnipeg Police Service; the percentage of Aboriginal constables was disproportionately small to the Aboriginal population of Winnipeg. However, Aboriginals were over-represented in the prison population at that time, as shown in the national statistics for 1990-91 for the percentage of the institutional population in terms of provincial and federal jails (see Table 1.1). The greatest over-representation was in the Prairie provinces, and in the two territories, Yukon and the Northwest Territories. For provincially run institutions, the percentage ranged from 35% in Alberta, to 49% in Manitoba to a peak of 68% in Saskatchewan. For federal institutions the range was from 31% in Alberta, to 39% in Manitoba to 52% in Saskatchewan. In the territories, which admittedly have a high percentage of Aboriginal people generally, the top numbers were 91% in the territorially run prisons in the Northwest Territories and 94% in the federally run prisons in Yukon (Frideres, 2001; 2012).

It should be noted that Manitoba had the second highest figures of any province in correctional institutions, both province and federal, second only to Saskatchewan. The Winnipeg area long made up a substantial part of that over-representation. Referring to statistics cited in a 1969 document titled, *Wahbung, Our Tomorrow*, written by the Manitoba In-

Table 1.1.
Aboriginal Inmates in Correctional Institutions by Region:
1990-1991

Region	Percentage of Provincial Instituion Population	Percentage of Federal Institution Population
Atlantic Provinces	3	3
Quebec	2	1
Ontario	8	4
Manitoba	49	39
Saskatchewan	68	52
Alberta	34	31
BC	18	14
NWT	91	37
Yukon	63	94

Source: Adapted from Frideres (2001, Table 5.3, p. 131); see also Frideres (2012, Table 4.13, p. 120).

dian Brotherhood, Comeau and Santin give a clear picture of Aboriginal over-representation in prison:

> Referring to a study of native offences and the number of native inmates in the province, the document noted that, in 1969, Indians made up about 4 per cent of Manitoba's population and just over 1 per cent in the Winnipeg area, but they accounted for 23 per cent of the 5,472 people involved in a variety of offences in the city and 19 per cent of the 4,302 held in Headingly Jail, half of whom were being held for failing to pay fines. (Comeau & Santin, 1990, p. 130)

Telling the Story

J.J. Harper was born in 1952 in the small northern Manitoban reserve community of Wasagamack First Nation,[2] a little more than 600 kilometres northeast of Winnipeg. Wasagamack First Nation is one of four descendant groups of the Island Lake band that signed onto Treaty Number Five in 1909, more than three decades after the less geographically and socially isolated groups did so. The language, Oji-Cree, a kind of blend of Ojibwe and Cree, is strong in the community,[3] so it would have been Harper's first language growing up, and English would have been his second language.

Harper became chief in 1982, when he was 30. The busy aspect of the job, particularly the travel to the three related bands and to Winnipeg, meant that he was often away from home. In 1984, he resigned, as his wife wanted him to spend more time with family. They decided to move to Winnipeg, where Harper went to work for the Island Lake Tribal Council. In less than half a year, he became its executive director in Winnipeg. Although at this time he was financially in the middle class, and was able to buy a house for himself, his wife, and their three children, all was not well with Harper and his family. There were arguments and there was drinking—his drinking. He moved out for most of the year but had moved back in. And he was Aboriginal, so he would not often have received the acceptance and respect of a white member of the middle class in Winnipeg.

The Crime and the Perpetrators

The case started with a simple, straightforward crime. Two young Aboriginal males, 19-year-old Melvin Pruden, who had a police record, and his 14-year-old cousin decided to steal a car and go joyriding. The crime was reported at about one o'clock in the morning, March 9. The car was observed, pursued, and forced to crash into a snow bank. The suspects were seen exiting the vehicle, and the police chased them on foot. The younger male was fairly quickly apprehended. After speaking with him, the following description of his cousin was broadcast across over police radio: "Male, Native, ah, black jacket, blue jeans…This male is approximately twenty-two years old" (Sinclair, 1999, p. 14). A later message presented the correct information, noting that the suspect's jacket and jeans were gray, and he had a "slim build."

J.J. Harper's Final Night

On the night of March 8, 1988, Harper had gone out on the town drinking with his friends. His wife was not with him, but that was not unusual. He had gone to several places, beginning at about 8:00 p.m. He first drank brandy and coffee at the St. Regis Hotel, talking and laughing with people he knew. At 10:30 p.m., he went to the Westbrook Hotel, and when the bar there closed, he went next door to a bar that was still open, finishing off with a few coffee-and-whiskies at a local tavern. At a blood alcohol concentration reading of 0.22, he was almost three times over the legal limit had he been driving, but he was walking home. His trip back home took him past a park in a working-class district of Winnipeg. While he was walking, the other perpetrator had been apprehended. Harper was walking in the general direction of the stolen car, which now rested in the snow bank. It was about 2:30 a.m., March 9th.

Harper then saw a white police officer, Robert Andrew Cross, walking toward him. At 33 years old, Cross was slightly younger than Harper. Cross saw an Aboriginal man with a stocky build wearing a black jacket and jeans. He did not accurately assess his age, or seem to think it important. He had about a minute before heard that a second suspect had been apprehended. Harper ignored Cross, as he had committed no crime, and probably had not developed the kind of positive relationship with the force that a white middle-class person would more likely have had. He probably had gone through a few experiences with the police that he would rather have not. The constable, who later admitted that he had a "slight suspicion" of Harper, but no reasonable and probable grounds upon which to arrest him (Hamilton & Sinclair, 1991, p. 38), asked him to show identification, and Harper refused, as was his legal right. The constable asked him again and Harper just kept walking away. The officer grabbed him by the arm and turned him around. Within a short period, Harper had been shot and was bleeding to death. By the time the ambulance arrived, picked him up, and delivered him to the hospital, J.J. Harper was dead.

We do not exactly know what happened that caused the discharge of the weapon. Cross claimed in court that Harper had pushed him down and tried to grab his gun. In the ensuing struggle, according to this story, the officer's finger found its way to the trigger as Harper was pulling on the barrel, and the gun accidentally went off.

Native in Appearance, Or "You Fit the Description"

In terms of the purposes of this book, the exact details of whether the officer was telling the truth and whether he had already drawn his weapon, as has been alleged, are relatively unimportant, compared to the following details:

a) A 36-year-old man, stocky with dark clothes, had been treated as a suspect for a crime that a radio message had attributed to a 22-year-old man with a slim build and gray clothes. Race trumped age, build, and clothing.

b) Racial differences between the Harper and Cross probably profoundly influenced the interaction between the two (as directed by both participants), leading to the deadly result. You do not have to be a sociologist to know that expectations are largely influenced by past experiences.

Both these key factors are a product of the personal history of experience of both men. The first comes in part from the "they all look the same to me" phenomenon often associated with people of East Asian heritage. Many of us have probably heard white people remark that they can't tell the difference between Chinese, Japanese, and Korean people.

The inability to distinguish, or think that distinguishing is important, comes to a significant extent from lack of experience. If you live in a big city, like to eat different foods, and go to Chinese, Japanese, and Korean restaurants, it shouldn't take you long to see differences between the peoples and their foods. The same could be true if you are a college or university professor and know the names of your Chinese, Japanese, and Korean students. It would be harder if you lived in a small town or the country, or if all or almost all of your colleagues at work are white. It is not part of your life experience to distinguish between these different groups of people.

My point here, which may be right or wrong for this individual case, is that had Cross had more experience with Aboriginal people in a broad variety of settings, including positive ones, not just on patrol and with Aboriginal offenders and potential suspects, and spent serious time with Aboriginal people as colleagues and equals, he probably would not have been so quick to mistake a middle-aged, middle-class, stocky Aboriginal person for a much younger, poorer and slimmer one, any more than he would be with white people that differ in the same ways. Although this is personal experience, it is conditioned by separations created by institutional racism.

Having had that broad experience with Aboriginal people may also have altered significantly how he treated Harper prior to the fatal shooting. He may have treated Harper with the same measure of respect that he would have a white, middle-class, middle-aged man who had been drinking but was walking home. But, to use a sociological term used earlier, "Indian" as master status overrides other statuses, such as class and age. When you add to that the idea that "adult Indian male out late at night equals criminal," you have a deadly situation.

This brings us to the phrase, "Native in appearance," which is the term recommended by the Winnipeg Police Service's *Departmental Procedures and Reporting Manual* to describe Aboriginal people. There is a great variety in how Aboriginal people look: young to old, tall to short, fat to thin, powerful to weak, long hair to buzz cut, well-dressed to shabbily dressed, blue-eyed or brown-eyed,[4] beautiful to plain, and relatively dark to relatively pale skin. In privileging that one phrase, the person giving the description can be encouraging police officers to believe that "all Indians look alike" and therefore that "all Indians match the description" and to ignore aspects of description that would discourage automatic apprehension of Aboriginal people (see Hamilton and Sinclair, 1991, p. 94).

Consider the phrase "**usual suspects**." The usual suspects are typically people who are "known to the police" for committing particular types of crimes, and who are automatically suspected of recently committed crime with which they are associated. Being "Indian" in Winnipeg, particularly at night, can put you in a situation in which you are treated as one of the usual suspects.

In one case, middle-class status of an Aboriginal driver had to be strikingly obvious to police officers in order to be recognized. You may have heard of young black males being picked up in Toronto or Halifax for DWB (Driving While Black). The following incidents can be termed DWA (Driving While Aboriginal) and RWA (Running While Aboriginal).

> A Winnipeg native told us that he drove a large car. If he was in blue jeans and an old sweater, the police regularly stopped him, questioned why he was driving such a big car, and how he could afford it. He wasn't allowed to go on his way until he proved he owned the car. On the other hand, he said that if he was wearing a suit and tie and driving the same care, he was never stopped or questioned.
>
> A young Aboriginal man told of being arrested and taken to the police station, for running down a city street. He explained to the police that he was late, and was running to meet his girlfriend, but he was not believed. He asked us to consider whether, if he had been white, he would have been apprehended. (Hamilton, 2001, p. 62)

Elizabeth Comack writes of a similar situation in which an Aboriginal high school student in Winnipeg who, because of an unstable family situation at home, was staying at a friend's place. Knowing that his friend's mother was going to ask him to leave soon, he was carrying three garbage bags late at night in which to carry his belongings. There had been a burglary nearby, and the police were looking for suspects. They apprehended him, and even though he had committed no prior offences (i.e., was a usual suspect in the usual way), the police

> took him to the District Station and charged him with possession of burglary instruments (the garbage

bags). His dad eventually retrieved him at 3:30 in the morning. In this case, being in possession of garbage bags on an inner-city street late at night was translated into a criminal offence in the judgment of the police officers involved. Had the Aboriginal youth been an older white man or woman walking down the same street at the same time of day, the incident might well have played out very differently. (Comack, 2012, p. 40)

The Scene of the Crime

Gordon Sinclair Jr., a journalist working for the Winnipeg Free Press, and author of *Cowboys and Indians: The Shooting of J.J. Harper*, wrote the following about what took place after Harper's death:

> Police wanted the scene cleaned up before day broke. There were three pools of blood, two large ones on the north sidewalk of Logan, and a splash on the narrow, curb-side boulevard. A detective, who had been assigned to make sure the clean-up was done properly, watched as the firefighters sloshed water on the three pools of blood and then covered them with sand. (Sinclair, 1999, p. 19)

Just as serious, in terms of the destruction of potentially important evidence, is that the gun was not dusted for fingerprints, as should have been done. Such evidence could have supported the officer's testimony (if Harper's prints were on the gun), or challenged it (if only Cross's prints were found). In the initial inquest, the lawyer employed by the police service said that the presence of Harper's fingerprints "would not be conclusive proof of anything" (Sinclair, 1999, p. 71), as he could have touched it accidentally, could have been trying to take the gun from Cross, or could have been trying to defend himself from being shot by Cross. While that is true, the responsibility and duty to collect all relevant evidence certainly must override such speculation. As it happens, fingerprinting of the gun did not take place until a week after the incident. The only visible print was that of the technician who had done the fingerprinting (Sinclair, 1999, p. 70).

In addition to that lapse of evidence collection, later that day, news reporters discovered Harper's glasses. The story told later was that the snow that had covered them the night before must have melted. They hadn't been found in any investigation of the scene. Further, the door-to-door search had been minimal. Add to that the fact that within 36 hours of Harper's death, the police chief said his officer was innocent of any wrongdoing and the mayor of Winnipeg agreed with him. The process was too hurried. This all speaks to the disposability of the person killed, his group, and his personal tragedy.

The Initial Inquest

The initial police report in the matter, made mandatory by the firing of a gun and by Harper's death, blamed Harper for his own death, as it was believed that he had assaulted Cross. The mayor of Winnipeg informed reporters that: "This is not a racial incident. It was just timing, circumstances and events" (Sinclair 1999, pp. 56-57).

In response to demands from Aboriginal leaders, on April 5, Judge John Enns of the Provincial Court of Manitoba headed an inquest into Harper's death. For a detailed and insightful telling of the story of that inquest, I encourage you to read the section in Sinclair's book entitled "The Inquest" (Sinclair, 1999, pp. 65-152). The inquest lasted until Enns's judicial statement was issued on May 26. His statement represented a mixture of views. On the one hand, Judge Enns expressed his belief that Cross's decision to question J.J. Harper could "easily be perceived as yet another instance of police harassment" (York, 1990, p. 151) to the Aboriginal leader. Enns acknowledged that Aboriginal people in Winnipeg had an "utter distrust" of the police, and he believed that the WPS should "vigorously pursue a program of recruiting natives" to help alleviate the tensions between the WPS and local Aboriginal people. However, when it came down to assigning blame, Enns felt that police harassment was more a "perception" than an actuality, and that Cross should be completely exonerated. That is easy to think and say when you have never had trouble with the police, never been treated as a potential criminal because of your race.

Aboriginal witnesses (the two suspects and three young women who had been in a car driving in the immediate area at the time) alleged that police in search of the suspects had their guns drawn, which the police denied. The suspects stated that the police had uttered racial remarks to them. But Aboriginal people as witnesses are suspect (if not suspects). In the words of journalist Don Gillmor, Judge Enns's logic seemed to follow a one-sided mistrust model.

> Allegations of racial slurs and allegations of drawn revolvers were not credible because the native witnesses were not credible. The natives were not credible because natives have an inherent mistrust of the police.
>
> However, that thinking did not work the other way: If racial slurs were made and guns were drawn, it would be indicative of the police's deep mistrust of the Aboriginal community. (Gillmor, 1988, p. 51)

That same mistrust of the Aboriginal community seems to have existed at the judicial level.

The Aboriginal Justice Inquiry (AJI)

In September 1988, in response to the handling of this case and the Helen Betty Osborne case, which we discuss in the next chapter, as well as a number of lesser known cases, the Aboriginal Justice Inquiry was established. It was not the only such inquiry of that time in Canada. In April of that year, a similar inquiry was held in Alberta, led by Provincial Court Judge Carl Rolf, with special emphasis on the bad relationships between mainstream police and the Kainai or Blood tribe in that province. Furthermore, published in 1988 by the Canadian Bar Association, *Locking up Natives in Canada*, by Professor Michael Jackson of the Faculty of Law at the University of British Columbia, presented a statistical study of the over-representation of Aboriginal people in the Canadian justice system.[5]

Judge Murray Sinclair

One of the commissioners for the AJI was Murray Sinclair. Sinclair was appointed associated chief judge of the

Provincial Court of Manitoba the month of J.J. Harper's death. He had been a lawyer since 1980, after studying several disciplines at the Universities of Manitoba and Winnipeg and acting as executive assistant to the provincial attorney general. He was the first Aboriginal person to be appointed a judge in Manitoba, the second one in Canada.

You can well imagine what some people would have thought of his appointment: "As he is an Aboriginal person he will be biased in his judgments." These prejudices might have biased some people in the WPS concerning Sinclair's work with the Manitoba Aboriginal Justice Inquiry. The truth is that, yes, he would have biases, as would any non-Aboriginal involved in the inquiry. There is the false impression that someone from the mainstream (i.e., a white judge) would be unbiased. This is a problem that has serious implications for Aboriginal justice. Potential jurors can be excluded if they are thought to have a bias that could prejudice the case. We will be exploring this idea in the chapter on Donald Marshall. The simple problem is that lawyers would find it easier to exclude potential Aboriginal jurors than white people on this count. Being completely objective with respect to people is impossible. Whatever job you do, you are affected in some way by your gender, race, ethnicity, age, class, and general life experiences.

Murray Sinclair comes from the Peguis First Nation (formerly known as the St. Peter's Indian Band), which is relatively close to Winnipeg, only about 145 kilometres north of Winnipeg. It is the largest band in Manitoba, with 9,394 registered members (Aboriginal Canada Portal, December 2012). Over the last few decades, the band has become one of the most "successful" Manitoba bands in mainstream economic terms. Peguis First Nation is very unlike Harper's home reserve in that a low percentage of people speak an Aboriginal language (2.4% spoke an Aboriginal language at home in 2006, most of these Saulteaux speakers, fewer Cree).

Murray Sinclair was profoundly influenced by his grandparents in his early years; they grounded him in the language of the Métis (Michif) and in the spiritual traditions of the Métis and Saulteaux. Interestingly, he also was very much what Henry Giroux calls a **border crosser** (Giroux, 2005), someone who can stand with knowledge and respect in more than one culture. His Métis grandmother raised him to be a Catholic, and he was involved with mainstream Canadian institutions such as the Boy Scouts and the Air Cadets. He did very well in high school; he was athlete of the year and class valedictorian in 1968.

In a piece published in AJI, Co-commissioner Alvin Hamilton's *A Feather Not a Gavel: Working Towards Aboriginal Justice*, Sinclair stated that his desire to become a lawyer came from wanting to change the situation of over-representation of his people in the jails and in criminal statistics, but he felt overwhelmed by two powerful thoughts. One was that the problem was too large for him to have an impact.

> The second thought–resulting from the manner in which we were taught about the glorious history of the common law–was that the problem of over-incarceration must be with Aboriginal people and not with anything the justice system was doing. It wasn't until many years later, as my legal career developed, and I had an opportunity to meet with many of the elders and wisdom keepers of the Aboriginal communities within which I worked as a lawyer, that I began to see my way past the second of those two thoughts. I found that what I had observed in law school was the end result of a long process of legalized racial oppression and political deprivation. (Sinclair as cited in Hamilton, 2001. p. 5)

After the AJI had done its work, in 1999 an Aboriginal Justice Implementation Commission (AJIC) was instituted to deal especially with those issues for which the government of the province of Manitoba was responsible. The commissioners were Paul L.A.H. Chartrand, a Manitoba Métis lawyer and university professor, and Wendy J. Whitecloud, a Manitoba Dakota lawyer. Their report was published in 2001.

Aboriginal Justice Inquiry and Its Recommendations

In 1991, the Aboriginal Justice Inquiry (AJI) made six specific recommendations specifically concerning the Winnipeg Police Service (then called the Winnipeg Police Department). First, they recommended that the WPS officially post, with the Winnipeg city council and the provincial minister of justice, an employment equity plan. This plan was to have clear, concrete targets concerning the number of Aboriginal officers that would be employed by the WPS, when those targets were to be achieved, and strategies or remedies that would be applied if those targets were not met on time.

Second, the first target set by the WPS in 1991 was one based on proportional representation. As it was estimated that Aboriginal people made up about 11.8% of the population of Manitoba, and there were 1,125 officers in the WPS by the end of 1990, they recommended that the concrete target set should be 133 Aboriginal officers. The number 133 became a quota, which can be construed as a "dirty word" to some non-Aboriginal people, both inside and outside the justice system.

There are two major complaints against the idea of quotas for the under-represented. One is that quota and quality are either/or situations; you have either one or the other. There are two opposing responses to such a complaint. One is that rigorous and reasonable standards be maintained (with no cynical hiring). The other is that the general quality of an organization such as a police service is raised by strengthening its diversity.

Another major complaint is that quotas represent "reverse discrimination," and any discrimination is wrong. Judge A.C. Hamilton heard that complaint in the AJI.

> I know there is criticism when a number of spaces are set aside for Aboriginal people. Three office workers berated me when the Winnipeg Police Service was making a number of positions available for qualified Aboriginal applicants. "What about my son?" one demanded. "Why should an Aboriginal person have a benefit he doesn't have?" (Hamilton, 2001, p. 113)

This kind of thinking seems to me to come from a false notion of an idealized "level or even playing field." If the system has a long tradition of a playing field sharply sloping in a way favourable to one group, any shift in the opposite direction towards the level will seem to be unreasonably sloped. Perhaps "reversing discrimination" might be a better term. In Judge Hamilton's words:

> Their criticism of preferential hiring might have had more merit if Aboriginal people had been participating on an even playing field for the last hundred years. If they had not been excluded from employment because of overt or systemic discrimination over the years, they would not need to catch up. (Hamilton, 2001, p. 113)

In addition, with the rest of the employment system still sloping against Aboriginal people in most areas, the "office worker's son" still has an advantage in terms of obtaining other jobs.

The AJI did a good job of establishing practical reasons for the quota. They listed 10 such reasons under the heading of "Advantages of Having Aboriginal Officers." The first advantage is that Aboriginal people will gain greater confidence to interact with the police. Second, Aboriginal officers would provide excellent role models for Aboriginal youth. While there initially might be some accusations from the youth that the officers are "Apples" (red on the outside and white on the inside[6]) or "Uncle Tomahawks," in the long run, particularly with the dramatic increase in Aboriginal police services ("tribal police") since the AJI report came out, the role model function should strengthen. An effective example of this kind of role modelling comes from the successful Kitigan Zibi Anishinabeg Police Department (KZAPD) (see Cummins & Steckley, 2003, pp. 123-125). They were one of four police forces, and the only Aboriginal-run force (the other three were in Toronto, Windsor, and Ottawa) to be engaged in a pilot project mentoring Aboriginal youth. Individuals from 12 to 24 were paired with police officers, riding in cruisers, observing police duties first-hand, visiting the homes of their police mentor, and travelling together for various outings. One KZAPD officer said, "I took great pride in seeing the barriers fall and the sense of openness that developed in our communication" (*First Nations Policing Update*, 1995). Police Chief Gordon MacGregor, then volunteering as a coach for the community's baseball team, in an interview with a reporter working for the federal Aboriginal Policing Directorate, stressed "the importance of being among the people, being visible and approachable especially to the youth and young children…People see you as being human and as a father, not just a police figure" (Stewart, 1996).

The third advantage was worded rather vaguely, stating that the "general population will benefit from seeing Aboriginal people in positions of responsibility, protecting the public peace." I see this in terms of decreasing tension in interaction between Aboriginal and non-Aboriginal people in the city. Anything that shows people are on "the same side" in terms of the law, that the division between Aboriginal and non-Aboriginal people is less than earlier imagined, as demonstrated by officers from the two groups working together, decreases racial tension. Anything that changes stereotyping increases understanding.

Fourth, Aboriginal officers would be good teachers to non-Aboriginal officers in terms of understanding Aboriginal culture and behaviour. What might appear threatening because it is different becomes less threatening when explained on the spot. Take, for example, Native drum groups (called generally "drums"). Even when these are performed in the context of a protest, with chanting that sounds threatening to the outsider and therefore potentially dangerous, an Aboriginal officer could explain the spiritual nature of most of the chants and how proud the drum groups feel in representing their traditions by drumming. Aboriginal youth engaged in drumming are not engaged in something illegal.

Aboriginal officers are advantageous to Aboriginal people who get arrested or who are the victims of crime, as they know what kind of Aboriginal community support is available to them.

Next, Aboriginal officers are important as translators. This might be obvious in a situation in which someone from a remote reserve is much more fluent in their native tongue (in Manitoba, most likely Cree, Saulteaux, Chipewyan or Dakota). Reserve English can also have its own unique twists and turns that could readily confuse a non-Aboriginal officer. Similarly, when an Aboriginal person wants to give a statement (either as suspect or witness), an Aboriginal police officer would be best able to insure that the true intent and meaning of what they want to say is reflected in the recorded statement. This has been a problem in the past. It should be noted here that in languages such as Cree and Saulteaux, there is no term for "guilty" but there is a term for "accuse."

Likewise, legalistic police/justice English (with its own twists and turns) could lead to confusion for an Aboriginal suspect, witness, or victim. Another advantage of having Aboriginal officers is that they are more likely to be able to insure that Aboriginal people understand what their rights are and what legal processes can take place. As much as many Aboriginal people have been over-represented in arrests and in prisons, such experiences do not necessarily ensure a clear understanding of the processes.

Another advantage of Aboriginal officers mentioned in the AJI report is that they exercise more preventive policing among members of the Aboriginal community in Winnipeg. They can establish contacts in that community where people can trust officers to talk about potentially dangerous or illegal situations before they happen. Also, they are able to determine whether an alternative means to arrest is possible, particularly when there is conflict between Aboriginal people.

The strategy for increasing the number of Aboriginal officers was to have the next class comprised entirely of Aboriginal recruits, with subsequent classes being 50% Aboriginal until the 133 quota was achieved. There was a huge mountain to climb as in 1990 there were only 18 Aboriginal officers. It would take roughly 15 years to meet the quota, as you can see from the statistics given below. In 2005, there were 134 Aboriginal officers. In terms of proportionate representation, it should be pointed out that in 2006, there were 137 Aboriginal police officers, or 10.6% of the officers were Aboriginal.

Aboriginal Representation Chart

Table 1.2 is derived from the annual reports of the WPS from 1997 to 2009. It includes the three equity groups of Caucasians or Whites, Aboriginal people, and Visible Minorities (Blacks, South Asians, Filipinos, Arabs, East Asians, and Chinese are typical examples in these charts). This part of the annual report (all of which is presented in the WPS

Table 1.2.
Winnipeg Police Service (WPS) Staffing by "Race" from 1997 to 2009

Year	Race	Sworn Constables	Civilian Staff	Change from Previous Year	
1997	Caucasian[7]	1,054	253	-	-
	Aboriginal	94	3	-	-
	Visible M.	42	14	-	-
	Total	1,190	270	-	-
1998	Caucasian	1,098	274	+44	+21
	Aboriginal	99	1	+5	-2
	Visible M.	44	13	+2	-1
	Total	1,241	288	+51	+18
1999	Caucasian	1,044	321	-54	+47
	Aboriginal	98	5	-1	+4
	Visible M.	43	17	-1	+4
	Total	1,185	343	-56	+55
2000	Caucasian	1,048	317	+4	-4
	Aboriginal	101	7	+3	+2
	Visible M.	46	17	+3	0
	Total	1,195	341	+10	-2
2001	Caucasian	1,029	324	-19	-19
	Aboriginal	104	9	+3	+2
	Visible M.	47	16	+1	-1
	Total	1,180	349	-15	+8
2002	Caucasian	1,047	335	+18	+11
	Aboriginal	108	10	+4	+1
	Visible M.	51	17	+4	+1
	Total	1,206	362	+26	+13
2003	Caucasian	1,073	339	+26	+4
	Aboriginal	109	11	+1	+1
	Visible M.	50	16	-1	-1
	Total	1,232	366	+26	+4

...continued

Table 1.2. continued

Year	Race	Sworn Constables	Civilian Staff	Change from Previous Year	
2004	Caucasian	1,068	339	-5	0
	Aboriginal	105	11	-4	0
	Visible M.	54	16	+4	0
	Total	1,227	366	-5	0
2005	Caucasian	948	315	-120*	-24
	Aboriginal	134	22	+29	+11
	Visible M.	158	21	+104*	+5
	Total	1,240	358	+13	-8
2006	Caucasian	1,076	368	+128*	+53
	Aboriginal	137	22	+3	0
	Visible M.	74	23	-84*	+2
	Total	1,287	413	+47	+55
2007	Caucasian	1,109	360	+33	-8
	Aboriginal	142	21	+5	-1
	Visible M.	75	25	+1	+2
	Total	1,326	406	+39	-7
2008	Caucasian	1,148	365	+39	+5
	Aboriginal	148	21	+6	0
	Visible M.	86	28	+11	+3
	Total	1,382	414	+56	+8
2009	Caucasian	1,169	362	+21	-3
	Aboriginal	151	22	+3	+1
	Visible M.	91	29	+5	+1
	Total	1,411	413	+29	-1

Source: http://www.winnipeg.ca/police/AnnualReports/annualreports/stm

website) was the manner in which the WPS responded to the third recommendation to report publicly the progress of their employment equity program.

There is an interesting anomaly in the figures for 2005 and 2006, which I have highlighted with an asterisk. It is enlightening to see the reaction of some of the non-Aboriginal and non-visible minority members of the WPS to measures that encouraged Aboriginal hiring. It seems very unlikely that 120 Caucasian officers were let go in 2005, with 128 hired back (or replaced by other Caucasian officers) the next year. Likewise, it is more than coincidence that the 2005 figure increased by 104 visible minorities, with a drop of 84 in 2006. It would appear that these confidential identity surveys were not answered accurately. It would seem, then, that there was some resistance to diversity initiatives on the part of many of the Caucasian officers of the Winnipeg Police Service. This is predictable and should be understood as natural. It does not necessarily mean that those who engaged in the resistance were racist. Imagine that you are made to feel that your ethnic identity is less significant than someone else's identity. The WPS would look better if your identity had a lower number and all other identities were higher. You are having a taste of institutional discrimination, a bitter taste of something that other identities have been forced to swallow for a much longer time. White people without significant power get to experience this taste while their leaders in the policing administration and in politics generally do not. In such cases, race plus class trumps mere race. Power is not fairly distributed, and you feel that lack of fairness. Resistance is understandable, however regrettable.

Considering the Civilian Members of the Winnipeg Police Service

Concern for the number of civilians working for the WPS was generally underplayed in the AJI report. There was no quota set up for civilians. In some senses there is good reason for the relative lack of time and effort spent in this area. First, the most immediate need was for Aboriginal officers "on the street."

Second, there is the danger of tokenism. Some civilian jobs could be easily perceived as token jobs as clerks. A

token involves a change more for the sake of appearance than for actual change in how a job is done or how a company works. An individual of a "designated group" is trotted out to be seen by visitors. It can be said that having a visual Aboriginal presence in a police station is a good thing, and it is. An all-white wall of humans can be intimidating to Aboriginal and visible minority suspects, victims, and complainants. However, the problem is that a token can be used in place of the real change. "Look, we don't have to change anything here; we have Aboriginal Andy as the office boy." The danger of tokenism would also apply with the hiring of only a few Aboriginal constables.

There is, however, an importance in having Aboriginal civilian employees. The following case shows that importance by demonstrating that not all front line work is done by sworn officers of the law.

Death by Neglect: The 911 Case

It was Friday evening, around 9 o'clock, February 15, 2000. Métis sisters Doreen Leclair and Corrine McKeown, aged 51 and 52 respectively, made five 911 calls to the Winnipeg police concerning the threatening presence of a former boyfriend. Eight hours later, the two women were found stabbed to death.

What happened? Regarding the first call, there is some dispute. Either the police didn't come, or they felt that nothing was amiss when an officer arrived there. No matter which version is true, by the third call, the women were seriously threatened. The tapes reveal that the women were telling the operator that a man violating a restraining order had stabbed Corrine. In response, the operator told the women that they were partially responsible for the situation in allowing the man into the house in the first place. Further, they should resolve the situation themselves.

A fourth call was made. The operator promised to send a squad car, but no such car was dispatched. Meanwhile, the situation escalated. Finally, by the fifth call, the operator became concerned, hung up the phone, and dialled the caller's number back. There was no response. When a police car was finally sent, it was too late to help.

A police-led investigation was held, during which four 911 operators and a duty inspector were suspended with pay. The resulting report was long in paper but short in addressing questions that local Aboriginal groups wanted answered. The next year, Manitoba's chief medical examiner called for an inquest. The Winnipeg Police Association opposed the inquest. The local police union president said that the main problems were there were too many 911 calls and too few officers hired to patrol the streets. The police chief admitted that the case was mishandled but denied that racism (at the personal level) or the lack of Aboriginal officers (i.e., institutional racism) played a part. It could well be that both personal and institutional racism were players in terms of the 911 operators. It is fairly certain that Aboriginal operators would have acted differently.

There was something else in play too: the stereotypes attached specifically to Aboriginal women. This theme will be picked up in the next chapter.

That year, as you can see from the chart presented above, there were only seven Aboriginal civilians working for the WPS. This represents roughly 2.2% of the civilians working for the service. By 2009, the number had more than tripled to 22, making up a still low 5.3%.

A fourth recommendation from the AJI was that a part of the funding provided by the provincial government to the municipal government of Winnipeg would be conditional on the WPS using that funding only for the hiring of Aboriginal police officers. This is using funding as a stick to punish non-compliance. Another strategy, more of a rewarding carrot than a stick, would be to make extra funding available for hiring Aboriginal recruits, like a NHL hockey player's performance-based bonus. The more Aboriginals are recruited, the more funding is provided.

The fifth recommendation had a different tone to it. We could call this recommendation the "non-ghettoization" recommendation. The idea was that the WPS should not automatically restrict Aboriginal police officers to the downtown core of Winnipeg, or to other areas that are disproportionately Aboriginal. I can think of various reasons why this is a good recommendation. For instance, the more experienced Caucasian police officers could socialize or teach the newly recruited Aboriginal officers the regular culture of policing when Aboriginal suspects are not involved. Fresh-out-of-school Aboriginal officers are still rookies who need to see how policing is usually done. Furthermore, Aboriginal police presence outside of "Aboriginal" areas demonstrates, particularly to white people, that Aboriginal officers are part of the team. Finally, it gives the Aboriginal police officers more scope than just "dealing with their own." Being pigeon-holed into one narrow context has restrictions in terms of the breadth of knowledge and future career prospects of new Aboriginal officers. The sense that "they are only fit to arrest their own kind" should not be allowed to develop.

The sixth recommendation was probably a very contentious one. I will introduce it with a term used in other social contexts: **credentialism**. This is the practice of valuing credentials–degrees, diplomas, certificates–over actual knowledge and ability in the hiring and promotion of staff.

One more term is necessary before we get to the specifics of Aboriginal recruitment. This term is prior learning assessment. If you access the website of the Canadian Association for Prior Learning Assessment (www.capla.ca), you will see that in Canada this idea first developed in eastern Ontario, where its principles and practices (e.g., challenge tests) were "nurtured" by conferences held and policies established at the First Nations Technical Institute beginning in the early 1990s. It involves the recognition of adult learning as set against the formal standards of the academic world (e.g., courses in specific subjects) and industry requirements for recruitment and promotion. A classic example that is a perpetual challenge in the Aboriginal educational world is Aboriginal language instruction. Typically, with most Aboriginal languages, the leading experts are fully fluent elders. But they don't have the paper credentials necessary to be permitted to teach in Aboriginal-run elementary and secondary schools that want provincial recognition for their courses. If prior learning assessment was fully practiced, then the elders' language expertise would hold greater credential weight.

How does this relate to the unstated sixth recommendation of the AJI? The commissioners recognized that one of the major roadblocks to recruitment of Aboriginal police officers was the grade 12 educational criterion. They suggested that the WPS develop "approaches which more appropriately test recruits' ability to perform the function required of police officers." This recommendation recognizes that a significant number of potential Aboriginal recruits are older than grade 12 graduates but have established a skill and knowledge set that is at least the equivalent of grade 12 through their work experience on reserves and elsewhere.

It is easy to see what kind of resistance there might be to this policy. This resistance takes the form of a kind of thinking in which attempts to broaden the racial, ethnic, class, or gender base of an organization are thought of as naturally being in opposition to "excellence." With this thinking, quota is believed to be in opposition to quality, and greater access being provided to an under-represented group becomes synonymous with "lowering standards." Another way of seeing this is to see that quotas for more diverse individuals provide a pathway to greater quality of the institution. In the same way, greater access of under-represented groups can provide a pathway to a redefined excellence, one that includes "diversity" in its definition. With more Aboriginal police officers in the WPS, it will deliver more effective policing, especially (but not exclusively) to Aboriginal people. Abolishing grade 12 as a form (the piece of paper delivered after going through and passing the courses in a classroom) but maintaining a standard of experiential equivalents will increase access and, if effectively executed, it will not lower standards. It would be unreasonable to put the long-term burden of this essentially educational issue on the backs of a policing service. That is one reason why the AJI also aimed to establish an Aboriginal Justice College, which would improve Aboriginal participation in the justice system and provide training for a broad range of jobs in the system, including court clerks, court administrators, court communicators or peacemakers (a unique Aboriginal position), probation officers, parole officers, custodial staff for local holding facilities and for jails, justices of the peace, and judges. Part of this proposed series of programs would be a pre-training or training of Aboriginal police officers. The importance of such an institution was reiterated 10 years later by the Aboriginal Justice Implementation Commission, which was appointed in November 1999 to review the recommendations made by the 1991 Report of the Aboriginal Justice Inquiry of Manitoba, and completed its work in a publication in 2001. By 2001, nothing substantial had been done to achieve this end.

Finally, in May 2008, the WPS, in partnership with the provincial government, announced the establishment of an "Indigenous Police Preparation Diploma." This is an eight-month program run through the University of Winnipeg. Funded by the federal government, the program was initiated by the RCMP and the Manitoba Métis Federation's Louis Riel Institute (the MMF's educational branch), which also provide guest speakers and elders in consultation with the Assembly of Manitoba Chiefs, Winnipeg Police Service, and Manitoba Justice. Classes began in September 2008. The program is not intended to duplicate training delivered at a police academy; rather, the idea is that it will ensure the success of Aboriginal candidates entering into police training programs. Interestingly, the program admission requirements include completion of grade 12. This could possibly reflect the increased success in high school education in Aboriginal populations over the 20 years since the institution of the AJI and the possibility that the mature, experienced potential recruits (without formal grade 12 education) were not as numerous as they were in 1991.

Cross-Cultural Training

Ignorance of Aboriginal people is widespread throughout Canada. This is not a unique feature of a police service (although police officers, as often straightforward speakers, may be more likely to articulate this shared ignorance in a loud, no-nonsense way). The AJI recognized this ignorance. As they stated:

> Most people in the justice system have little understanding of Aboriginal people, their history, culture, or way of life. Our study has convinced us that there are widespread misconceptions about Aboriginal people and about their perception of the law and legal system. (AJIC, Final report, chapter 12)

This being the case, they strongly recommended that cross-cultural training be implemented for members of the justice system. With respect to police, the recommendations included:

- Cross-cultural education components of all police training courses be reviewed and strengthened, and this process actively involve members of the Aboriginal community, resource persons and recognized experts.

- All police officers be rotated through cross-cultural education programs, and periodic refresher programs be provided as part of the regular professional development programs of all police departments. (AJIC, 2001, p. 114)

The Aboriginal Justice Implementation Commission took this one stage farther, recommending that: "the Government of Manitoba adopt a policy that prefers Aboriginal people to deliver cross-cultural training programs."

Another reason, other than the demonstration effect, for suggesting that Aboriginal people should deliver the cross-cultural training is that a non-Aboriginal expert is more likely to engage in traditional classroom lecturing techniques, even engaging in some largely unintentional "preaching," whereas Aboriginal people would have a higher likelihood of teaching through experiences shared both inside a classroom and outside of it. It is the latter that is particularly important. Experiencing the culture, when supported with classroom explanations and questions and answers, can provide more in-depth and real world training. This is particularly the case when elders are involved. Stories and cultural demonstrations of skills are best told where an elder is most comfortable. The classroom is not as much a home to them (particularly if they had residential school experience) as it is to non-Aboriginal experts.

Changing the Chiefs

Significant changes in a police service require a shift in the culture of the institution. The chief of a service, particularly one who rose up within the ranks to reach the top, epitomizes the institutional culture, which is an impediment to change. Chief Herb Stephen of the WPS seriously opposed the idea of quotas. As the AJI report stated:

> Chief Stephen told us he is opposed to the use of quotas. The use of quotas is a well-recognized means of ensuring that employment equity programs achieve results and are not merely public relations exercises. But Stephen said that he believed that every recruit or applicant must compete for the available spaces. The current procedure is that if two applicants are considered to be equally qualified, preference may be given to the Aboriginal applicant. From what we heard about the selection criteria, we doubt if the present system will allow any Aboriginal applicants to be considered equal in every category with other applicants. (AJIC, Final report, chapter 11)

The chief, who was also opposed to any flexibility in the education requirement, retired in 1991. The WPS then took two unusual steps. One was to have no chief, having the two deputies share the tasks. Following that, they brought in, from the RCMP 'D' Division, the former head of the WPS. It was the first time that the chief was not someone who came up from within the ranks.

In 1996, they went back to the usual methods, hiring David Cassels, the same year that the Aboriginal Advisory Committee was initiated. He was replaced in 1998 by the current (2012) chief.

Conclusions

The death of J.J. Harper in 1988 was the result of an intolerable situation for Aboriginal people in the justice system in Winnipeg, Manitoba, and in Canada in general. A precedent-setting investigation, the Aboriginal Justice Inquiry (AJI), and a series of follow-up measures were directed to changing this situation. In looking over this chapter, and addressing the questions below, the reader is invited to understand the improvements and the remaining challenges to assess how conditions have changed for the better.

The negative contact of urban Aboriginal people and the law continues to exist, as does the distrust of the criminal justice system. A 2010 Environics Institute study found that nearly two-thirds of urban Aboriginal people had some serious contact with the criminal justice system at some point in their lifetime. That is, they had been charged or arrested or had been witnesses to crimes. More than half of the urban Aboriginal people surveyed stated that they had little or no confidence in the criminal justice system. That is around twice as many as would be found in a comparable study of non-Aboriginal Canadians (see Frideres & Gadacz, 2012, p. 139).

Questions

1. Do you think that the number of Aboriginal officers has risen sufficiently to prevent another J.J. Harper incident from taking place?
2. What else might need to be done to ensure that such an incident does not take place?
3. How do you think the figures relate to the often repeated false statement that "no police service is hiring white people anymore"?
4. When the police chief was asked for a comment, he claimed that he had never seen an incident of racial harassment in all of his 32 years on the police force. He went on to say: "All of a sudden, boom, this comes up and there's a racial problem" (Sinclair, 1999, p. 58). Why was this both an accurate assessment of what he was able to "see" as well as an inaccurate statement of the situation he was viewing?
5. What qualities and experiences would make Judge Murray Sinclair an ideal candidate for the position of commissioner of the AJI?
6. Would a carrot approach of additional funding for the hiring of Aboriginal police officers be more effective than the stick approach of making part of existing funding conditional upon meeting a specific quota? Would a combined approach be better?
7. Should Aboriginal police officers be restricted to the downtown core and other Aboriginal areas of the city of Winnipeg? What problems might exist in trying to implement such a policy?

8. Why is it beneficial to have Aboriginal people lead cross-cultural courses?
9. How would changing the regime help to change the culture in the WPS? Could change occur any other way?
10. Do you think that a situation such as the death of J.J. Harper would be likely to occur again in the twenty-first century? Why? Why not?

Key Terms

border crosser–a person who is experienced, knowledgeable, and comfortable in both sides of an ethnic or racial border (e.g., Aboriginal and mainstream Canadian).

credentialism–the practice of considering primarily or solely the possession of paper credentials (e.g., high school diplomas, post-secondary courses, diplomas, or degrees) with insufficient consideration of other ways in which that knowledge or skillset is achieved.

institutional or systemic racism–a situation in which policies, practices, and beliefs operate in organizations in such ways as to actively discriminate against one or more racialized groups.

master status–the socially recognized position or condition (e.g., police chief, Aboriginal person, mother, disabled person, alcoholic, or queen) a person holds that is considered either by the individual, significant groups, and society in general to be the one that primarily defines who that person is.

over-representation–a situation in which a group's percentage presence in an organization, an occupation, or a situation is significantly higher than their percentage of the total population (e.g., white males as federal cabinet ministers and Aboriginal people in Canadian prisons).

personal racism–a situation in which an individual's personal views and actions show clear prejudice and discrimination.

prior learning assessment–a practice of determining whether an individual's accumulated experience and knowledge can be deemed equal to that of a course, level, or credential recognized by the education system.

status–a socially recognized position or situation held by an individual (e.g., father, teacher, dentist, African-Canadian, and disabled person). Several statuses can be held at the same time.

status inconsistency–a situation in which the rankings (i.e., high or low) of an individual's situation do not align (i.e., some are ranked significantly higher or lower than the others).

token–someone of an under-represented group who is placed in a highly visible position so that he or she gives the appearance that an organization does not discriminate against that group.

under-representation–a situation in which a group's percentage presence in an organization, occupation, or situation is significantly lower than that groups percentage of the total population.

usual suspects–people who are usually "known to the police" for committing particular types of crimes, and who are automatically suspected of recently committed crime with which they are associated. In a racialized situation, this term expands to include racialized people who share a race with the perpetrators.

Notes

[1] Boycotts happen with every census. This resistance comes essentially from an Aboriginal distrust of federal governments. Fortunately, for governmental officials, statisticians, and sociologists, the number of bands that actively boycott the census declined in the 2006 and 2011 censuses.

[2] On the Government of Canada's Aboriginal Canada Portal, accessed January 11, 2013, it was reported that, as of December 2012, the band's populations was 1,919 with 1,740 on reserve (a high percentage in comparison to many other bands) (www.aboriginalcanada.gc.ca/acp/community/site.nsf/eng/fn29).

[3] The 2006 census indicated that of respondents from this community, 93.1% said Oji-Cree was the language they first learned and 94.8% said it was spoken in the home. This is unusually high, even for a Cree community.

4   The thirteen-year-old suspect alleged that Cross's partner called him "a blue-eyed fucking Indian" (Comack, 2012, p. 82).

5   This document was later published in 1989 in the *University of British Columbia Law Review*, 23(2), 215-300.

6   Aboriginal people are not actually red, more different shades of brown. The idea that they are red came from the use of red ochre, an earth dye, among the Beothuk of Newfoundland and other eastern peoples early contacted by Europeans.

7   Caucasian is the more formal term used to refer to "white people." It owes its origin to the early biological race-based notion that the "purest" or most typical examples of white people came from the area of the Caucasus Mountains in Russia. When I was a boy, and watched a lot of police shows on television, I first thought that Caucasians were some kind of criminal.

References

Aboriginal Canada Portal. Retrieved from http://www.aboriginalcanada.gc.ca

Aboriginal Justice Implementation Commission (Paul L.A.H. Chartrand & Wendy J. Whitecloud, Commissioners). (2001). Aboriginal employment and participation in the justice system (Chapter 8). Winnipeg: Government of Manitoba. Retrieved from http://www.ajic.mb.ca/reports/final_ch08.html

Aboriginal Justice Implementation Commission (Paul L.A.H. Chartrand & Wendy J. Whitecloud, Commissioners). (2001). The police and Aboriginal people (chapter 11). Retrieved from http://www.ajic.mb.ca/volume lll/chapter11.html

Aboriginal Justice Implementation Commission (Paul L.A.H. Chartrand & Wendy J. Whitecloud, Commissioners). (2001). Strengthening communities. Retrieved from http://www.ajic.mb.ca/reports/final_ch12.html

Aboriginal People in Manitoba. (2006). Winnipeg, MB: Her Majesty the Queen in Right of Canada. Retrieved from http://www.gov.mb.ca/ana/pdf/apm2006.pdf

Comack, E. (2012). The shooting of J.J. Harper. In *Racialized policing: Aboriginal People's encounters with the police* (pp. 89-114). Halifax: Fernwood Publishing.

Comeau, P., & Santin, A. (1990). *The First Nations: A profile of Canada's Native People today.* Toronto, ON: James Lorimer and Company.

Cummins, B.D., & Steckley, J.L. (2003). *Aboriginal policing: A Canadian perspective,* Toronto, ON: Pearson Canada.

Environics Institute. (2010). *Urban Aboriginal Peoples study.* Retrieved from http://www.uaps.ca

First Nations Policing Update. (1995, July, no. 3.) Aboriginal Policing Directorate, Solicitor General Canada. Catalogue no. JS42-58/3-1995.

Frideres, J.S. (1998). Aboriginal Peoples in Canada (5th ed.). Scarborough, ON: Prentice-Hall.

Frideres, J.S. & Gadacz, R.R. (2012). *Aboriginal Peoples in Canada* (9th ed.). Toronto, ON: Pearson Canada.

Gillmor, D. (1988). The Shooting of J.J. Harper. *Saturday Night,* December.

Giroux, H. (2005). *Border crossings: Cultural workers and the politics of education.* New York, NY: Routledge.

Hamilton, A.C. (2001). *A feather not a gavel: Working towards Aboriginal Justice.* Winnipeg, MA. Great Plains Publications.

Hamilton, A.C. & Sinclair, C.M. (1991). Report of the Aboriginal justice inquiry of Manitoba. *The deaths of Helen Betty Osborne and John Joseph Harper* (Vol. 2). Winnipeg, MB: Queen's Printer.

Jackson, M. (1989). *Locking up Natives in Canada.* Ottawa, ON: Canadian Bar Association.

Lee, J.A. (1983). Controlling society. In J.P. Grayson (Ed.). *Introduction to sociology: An alternate approach.* Toronto, ON: Gage Publications.

MacKinnon, S. (2009). Tracking poverty in Winnipeg's inner city (pp. 27-36). In S. Mackinnon & J. Brody (Eds.). *State of the inner city.* Winnipeg, MB: Canadian Centre for Policy Alternatives.

Sinclair Jr., G. (1999). *Cowboys and Indians: The shooting of J.J. Harper.* Toronto, ON: McClelland & Stewart.

Stewart, S. (1996, March). A day in the life of two community police officers: The Aboriginal Police directorate takes a look at the First Nations policing policy in action. *First Nations Policing Update,* No. 4.

York, G. (1990). *The dispossessed: Life and death in Native Canada.* London: Vintage.

Chapter 2

The Helen Betty Osborne Case

People still ask me, "Come on, did everyone really know who the killers were?" and I said, "Yeah, we all knew but we didn't say anything." (Priest, 1989, frontispiece)

The writers of the *Report of the Aboriginal Inquiry of Manitoba* summed up the Helen Betty Osborne case well when they described Osborne as a victim of

> vicious stereotypes born of ignorance and aggression when she was picked up by four drunken men looking for sex. Her attackers seemed to be operating on the assumption that Aboriginal women were promiscuous and open to enticement through alcohol or violence. It is evident that the men who abducted Osborne believed that young Aboriginal women were objects with no human value beyond sexual gratification. (as cited in Acoose, 1995, p. 70)

Writing about the virtually anonymous Canadian serial killer John Martin Crawford, author Warren Goulding stated:

> As of this writing Crawford has been convicted of four deaths, all of them women, all of them Native. He is also a suspect in at least three other murders or mysterious disappearances of aboriginal women in Saskatoon. But Crawford has been the beneficiary of a disinterested media and an equally impassive public. More important, his victims have suffered even

further because of this indifference. (Goulding, 2001, p. xiii)

The sister of the first Aboriginal woman killed by Crawford articulated the following sad statement:

It seems any time a Native is murdered...it isn't a major case. It's just another dead Indian. (Goulding, 2001, p. xv)

Aboriginal author Janice Acoose, writing in late 1994, when the remains of four Aboriginal women had recently been found on the outskirts of Saskatoon, expressed the following concerning the mainstream response to the discoveries and the deaths:

I have waited in agonized and frustrated silence for some kind of expression of concern (perhaps even outrage) from members of the community, women's groups, or political organizations. To date few, if any, have come forward and spoken to the nature of this heinous crime, or the need to protect Indigenous women who were so obviously the targets of the murderer. And, perhaps more importantly, I waited for someone to come forward and respectfully acknowledge the lives of these four young women. Their existence on this earth has not been respectfully eulogized in the press in the same way that other murder victim's lives have been. (Acoose, 1995, p. 86)

In a 2011 interview, Cree scholar and writer Robyn Bourgeois talked about how the myth of the Aboriginal woman as a sexual deviant persists:

The myth of the deviant Aboriginal woman continues to plague us, reinforced by dominant cases that coalesce prostitution and Aboriginal women into a single entity. Contemporary Canadian society dismisses violence against Aboriginal women and girls today on the basis of these perceived deviances (addicted, sexually available). We are not even treated as human beings. Human beings have the right to a life free from violence, yet we have to convince the Canadian state to step up and protect us. And these stereotypes provide the justification for why the State doesn't step up. (*Black Coffee Poet*)

The Helen Betty Osborne Case

The Helen Betty Osborne case is an important one for the Canadian justice system, both in itself, but also as an illustration of how a stereotype and a position of vulnerability can lead to the death of a growing number of young Aboriginal women. While the case has been legally dealt with, the problems it highlights are far from being resolved. Learning from this case, and from others like it, is necessary to stop violence against Aboriginal women.

The sociological literature informs us that race and gender can intersect as forms of oppression to create a greatly targeted object of oppression, a kind of multiplier effect. The sociological term for this phenomenon is **intersectionality.** Racial prejudice and discrimination can often reinforce gender bias, and vice versa. In the case of Aboriginal women, this has come together in the negative image of the **squaw.** The case of Helen Betty Osborne illustrates well the effects of intersectionality.

The Squaw: The Negative Stereotype of Aboriginal Women

> The portrayal of the squaw is one of the most degrading, most despised and most dehumanizing anywhere in the world. The squaw is the female counterpart of the Indian male savage and, as such, she has no human face. She is lustful, immoral, unfeeling and dirty. (Donna Sears, as quoted in the Royal Commission on Aboriginal People)

What is a squaw? The now derogatory term squaw developed innocently enough from a word in the Massachusetts (as an Aboriginal group not a state) language meaning female. There are related terms in a number of Canadian Aboriginal languages that belong to what linguists call the Algonquian language family, the largest Aboriginal language family in Canada and the United States. Its traditional use can be seen in examples from the Ojibwe (called variously Anishinabe, Algonquin, Mississauga, Chippewa, or Saulteaux) language, in which the *s* is dropped to give us *kwe*, which can be a word by itself or as part of a word (bolded below):

kwe	woman	(Rhodes, 1985, p. 619)
kwe*wag*	women	(Rhodes, 1985, p. 210)
kwe*zens*	girl (little woman)	(Rhodes, 1985, p. 484)

A nineteenth-century Mississauga from the Credit River area of southern Ontario (see Steckley, 1999) bore the Ojibwe name Nahnebahwequay, which means "Standing up Woman" (the *quay* representing *kwe*).

How did this straightforward non-judgemental term of reference to females change into something negative? When European explorers and traders first came into contact with Aboriginal people in Canada and the United States, they encountered women from cultures that were generally not as restrictive or condemning with respect to sex outside of marriage. It would be easy for such men to apply the "if you were in my culture, then you would be judged negatively as promiscuous" to mean "you must be promiscuous."

In addition, the hardworking life of the Aboriginal woman in her own culture was often presented by early writers in a negative light, typically misleadingly so. A classic example of this is the following story related to Chipewyan women, the Chipewyan being a people who live in the Northwest Territories and the northern stretches of Manitoba, Saskatchewan, and Alberta. Writer Simon Hearne reflects on his trip across northern Canada from 1769 to 1772. His unreliable distorting source for this commentary was the Chipewyan man Matonnabbee, whose dependence on the European trading post and traders (and not his people) for his relatively prominent position at the time had led him to acquire seven wives (a number not in keeping with traditional practices) whom he appears to have exploited to an extreme. Believing that his opinion reflected traditional Aboriginal practice might be like accepting a marriage manual written by Henry VIII (who executed wives that did not produce sons).

Women…were made for labour; one of them can carry, or haul, as much as two men can do. They also pitch our tents, make and mend our clothing, keep us warm at night; and, in fact, there is no such thing as travelling any considerable distance, or for any length of time, in this country, without their assistance. Women…though they do everything, are maintained at a trifling expence (sic); for as they always stand cook, the very licking of their fingers in scarce times, is sufficient for this subsistence. (Hearne, 1958, p. 35; see Steckley, 1999, pp. 88-90 for a more complete discussion of this man)

Add to these factors the harsh conditions the women had to endure when many of their men, from the late eighteenth throughout the nineteenth century, were affected by the massive amounts of alcohol poured into the fur trade (see the Minnie Sutherland chapter), and the negative conditions brought about when wide ranging territories were replaced by more confining and less resource rich reserves, particularly in the Canadian prairies, and you have an image of a sexual object and a slaving drudge that becomes attached to the term and concept squaw. As Klein and Ackerman explain,

The concept of "squaw" belittles the lives of Native men and women alike. The squaw is a drudge who is forced to endure hard work while her husband swaps hunting stories with his friends….[T]he Native woman appears to have no social input, no choice in spouses, and no respect. She is an inferior to her husband and necessary only for her labor and for her sexual and reproductive duties. Her sexual favors can be sold by her husband while she meekly acquiesces (Klein and Ackerman, 1995, p. 5)

Remember that this image is more fiction that fact, more distorting stereotype than actuality. Think of how easy it is to re-inforce a stereotype with a small example than it is to break one with a broader truth.

In the town of The Pas, where Helen Betty Osborne for a short time lived, the stereotype would have readily visible reinforcement for white men on the prowl, as we will see shortly. They did not get to see the many more Aboriginal women who were strong and important players in their communities.

In part, this was because of the **gendering** effect of the laws put in place by federal governments since the late nineteenth century. Gendering in this context refers to changing the gender roles and rules in a particular group (in this case Aboriginal people) to more closely match those in another (i.e., that of mainstream Canadian society in the nineteenth century). Women traditionally could have real authority in Aboriginal society. You can see this in the historical record of the Wyandot of the Detroit/Windsor area in the eighteenth century. In 1747, they had an elders' council that was highly involved in decision making of the people. There were 60 members of this council. Twenty-nine of them were women. The Wyandot were also **matrilineal**, meaning that they determined kinship primarily along the mother's or female line. A number of Canadian First Nations determined kinship in that way. Further, when treaties were signed by a number of different Aboriginal people in Canada, the term "principal women" (see Steckley, 1999, pp. 147–148 for a Mississauga example) was not uncommon. Facts such as these tell you something of the respect in which women were held.

The Abuse of Aboriginal Women by the Indian Act

Federal law through the **Indian Act** (formally passed in 1876), which created the political existence of band chiefs and councils, did not initially let women vote (as women did not have the vote in mainstream Canada) or run for office:

> At the election of a chief or chiefs, or the granting of any ordinary consent required of a band of Indians under the Act, those entitled to vote at the council or meeting thereof shall be the male members of the band of the full age of twenty-one years. (Indian Act, 1876 Section 61)

It was not until 1951 that Aboriginal women could vote or run for office in band elections for chief or council. In one of those strange twists of fate, the first Aboriginal woman to become a chief of a First Nation band was Jean Folster (1922-1994), who became the chief of Norway House Cree Nation, Helen Betty Osborne's home reserve community, in 1971, the same year that Osborne was murdered. Both women have institutions named after them in that community. Folster has a women's shelter that takes her name; a local school bears Osborne's name.

Furthermore, if an Aboriginal woman who was a **status Indian** married a man who was not a status Indian, she would lose her status and could, conceivably, be kicked out of the reserve of her people. This regulation would change to a certain extent with the passage in 1985 of **Bill C-31**, which allowed women and some of their descendants who had lost their status in that way to regain it. It was limited in creating male and female equality on reserves as the band government of chief and council was permitted to determine who were and were not band members with rights related to being able to live on the reserve. As sociologist James Frideres notes, this power (and women) have been abused by the mostly male band chiefs and councillors who have chosen to exclude people (mostly women) given Indian status by Bill C-31 (Frideres & Gadacz, 2012, pp. 149-150). The law still perpetuates a sexist bias.

Bill C-31 was still in the future when the killing of Helen Betty Osborne took place. Women had lost their traditional status and did not then often have the positions of official power (i.e., chief or councillor) that outsiders would see leadership in. Certainly, the quietly strong and important female figures in the local Aboriginal communities such as Norway House would not be seen by the white people of The Pas, even if they were standing right in front of them. The strong figure of Jean Folster would not be conjured up in their minds.

The Pas in 1971: The Mudlarks

The Pas is a northern Manitoban town. The name comes from the Cree word *w'passkwayaw*, meaning "where the river narrows." It was shortened to Opasquia, then to The Pas. In 1971, the town was a pulp and paper boomtown, with a population rising about 6,000 and growing. There were also profitable mining operations not far to the north. This meant that there would be a lot of unattached men moving into the area, men with more money than they had ever had before and few responsibilities that would divert that money to practical family ends. Alcohol, drugs, and women would be high on their list of spending priorities. And the women who were most available were Aboriginal street women, women who were easily considered disposable. There are two descriptions of these women that I want you to read, one comes from the chapter entitled "The Mudlarks" (pp. 144-165) in Heather Robertson's work, *Reservations Are for Indians*. She is writing about the women who hung around outside the main bar in downtown The Pas, The Gateway Hotel.

> They are the mudlarks. They linger on the fringe waiting, watching. If one of them is lucky, some man will come along buy her a beer or two inside and take her to a flophouse around the corner for the night. She might stay with this man for a week or a year; she might be beaten and thrown out on the street in the morning. The mudlarks live on the streets of The Pas, scavenging what they can. They have no homes; their families have disintegrated or don't want them because they cost too much to feed.
>
> These pathetic little dark girls are not seductive, bundled up against the cold in ski pants and ugly nylon jackets, shivering. They are hardly noticeable, all dressed in drab black, hiding in the shadows. Skinny and bony, their faces are hard and lined already, dry and dull-eyed. Their hair is lank, dirty, and their efforts at soliciting clumsy and childish....It is not really accurate to call these women and girls prostitutes. There is so little money involved and they are so apologetic, unassuming, and unprofessional, they will go with a man for nothing, just on a gamble that something will turn up. (Robertson, 1970, p. 145)

Lisa Priest's description in *Conspiracy of Silence* is also quite telling in a powerful journalistic way.

> They were malnourished, with dried eyes, prematurely wrinkled faces, and round bellies...They stood leaning sloppily to one side...[A]ll were helpless be-

cause they had nowhere to sleep except under the railroad bridge and nowhere to work, except maybe The Gateway. Some of them would settle for a glass of beer from any man who cared to offer one, hoping to find a warm place at the end of night, whether it was the flophouse around the corner from The Gateway or the back seat of a car. (Priest, 1989, p. 49)

Here the vital crime prevention role of the police is rather conspicuous by its absence. In a way, you could say that the situation in which the Helen Betty Osborne case emerged was a murder waiting to happen. This was identified in the Aboriginal Justice Inquiry report as follows:

> We know that cruising for sex was a common practice in The Pas in 1971. We know too that young Aboriginal women, often underage, were the usual objects of the practice. And we know that the RCMP did not feel that the practice necessitated any particular vigilance on its part. (http://www.ajic.mb.ca/volumeII/chapter 5.html)

Vigilance by the police was necessary to protect the young Aboriginal female citizens of the area. By condoning by their relatively casual non-opposition of the practice of the sexual exploitation of Aboriginal women, the police were contributing to the prejudiced attitude towards and unsafe situations lived by young Aboriginal women. The police were part of the problem, when they could have been part of the solution.

Racialized Spaces

The concept of **racialized space** refers to public areas that, according to the local or general culture, are considered to "belong" to a particular racialized group to the general exclusion of other groups. And if racialized group is generally negatively valued, then those found in the racialized space are assumed to be causing trouble. A number of the inner city neighbourhoods in Winnipeg are considered "Aboriginal space." If you are male, you are generally assumed by the police to be a gang member, a thief, and a drug dealer. Unfortunately for Aboriginal women, when they are found in this racialized space at night, the assumption is that they are prostitutes, and they are often treated accordingly. The streets of The Pas were similarly racialized at night for Helen Betty Osborne. As she was in that space at that time and an Aboriginal female, she was considered a prostitute.

Elizabeth Comack provides us with examples of this kind of racialized space with Aboriginal women she had interviewed. Dianne, in her early twenties in the winter of 2008, had been visiting her uncle in downtown Winnipeg. On her way home, she walked towards a phone booth to call her dad to ask for a ride the rest of the way home. A police vehicle pulled up beside her and the officers proceeded to charge her with prostitution: "They said I was standing around trying to work the streets...They grabbed me and they handcuffed me...the cops said that they saw me going to a car, which I wasn't. I was going to the pay phone" (Comack, 2012, p. 166). Helen Betty Osborne would die because she was walking in racialized space.

Helen Betty Osborne

Helen Betty Osborne came from Norway House Cree Nation. At the time that she left it, the double community of village and reserve comprised about 1,700 Cree, 700 Métis, and 250 white people. She lived in a crowded house that would fit the picture of what many non-Aboriginal people think of what reserve life is like, particularly after seeing the conditions of Attawapiskat in Northern Ontario on television and in print media in 2011 and 2012. She was determined to leave that kind of life by becoming educated, but she did not want to leave her community, to which she was emotionally attached.

If you want to read a depressing version of what life was like during the days in which Helen Betty Osborne was growing up, read chapter four "Norway House" of Heather Robertson's 1970 classic, *Reservations Are for Indians*. While it captures much of what a non-Aboriginal outsider can see in the community, it does not show the inner strength that is often found in places such as Norway House, the kind of strength that Helen Betty Osborne seemed to have.

The Killing of Helen Betty Osborne

On a cold northern Manitoban night, November 12, 1971, a young white man, 18-year-old Lee Colgan, got his father's car and drove down to the Cambrian Hotel, where he picked up three friends: Dwayne Johnston (18), Norman Manger (25), and James Houghton (23). They had one of the ingredients of a standard good time in The Pas: alcohol. So, for several hours they motored and drank. Colgan became so drunk and was driving so erratically that, even by the relatively slack drinking and driving standards of the time, he considered himself unable to drive and Houghton took the wheel.

What they wanted now were women to "party" with, or at least one willing woman to party with all four of them. What they wanted was a squaw. Then they saw a short, slight "Indian" woman, a "squaw," walking along a poorly lit street in the downtown area. Her name, although they would not have known it, was Helen Betty Osborne.

Helen was a 19-year-old Cree woman, speaker of the Swampy Cree dialect as well as   English with ambitions to rise above the overcrowded living conditions in which her family lived in her Norway House reserve community. To do this she needed an education, become something, a nurse perhaps or a teacher to return to help her home community, as so many educated Aboriginal people long to do. To get that education, she needed to go to high school in The Pas. There were no high schools in her community. Once she graduated from high school, who knows what she could achieve? She liked school, and she showed promise. She had potential for a good future.

There was a program of education **desegregation** then being initiated through the federal government, which was not unlike the few years-old policy that bussed in black students to previously all-white schools in the American South.

Segregation, the separation of the lives of the two different peoples in the community, was a well-established discriminatory practice in The Pas in 1971. White people and Aboriginal people even had to sit on opposite sides of the town movie theatre. Ushers would tell Aboriginal people to move to their own side if this rule was violated. It was also noted by the Aboriginal Justice Inquiry that similar segregation existed in restaurants, local drinking establishments, and even in the cafeteria in the high school that Helen attended.

In an effort to end educational segregation, the Department of Indian Affairs (DIA) paid for room and board for the white families that would put up an Aboriginal student, and gave money on a per-student basis to the local high school Margaret Barbour Collegiate Institute. The conditions were not ideal, as with any such policy that came from the outside. While the school now (2012) provides three different courses in Aboriginal studies, one can be fairly certain there were no such courses then in which understanding of and respect for Aboriginal culture were promoted. Mainstream culture was the sole offering to students, white or Aboriginal. Homesick, victims of slight and larger incidents of personal racism, and not familiar with the formal English of the mainstream classroom, many Aboriginal students returned home without educational success. Helen, however, was succeeding, slowly but surely. She failed one year, but was determined to see her way through to completion. After news of Helen's death, many Aboriginal parents pulled their children out of the program. Girls that remained were encouraged to always walk in pairs. They were not safe alone in The Pas.

Osborne had Aboriginal friends in town and was competing with a few other girls to be the girlfriend of a particular young Aboriginal man (who would be the first suspect that the police would question about her murder). She did not particularly like white boys. A female friend of hers from Norway House claimed, "She couldn't understand why some Indian women liked White men when she didn't…She always said she would marry and Indian man" (Priest, 1989, p. 23). Further, she was generally afraid of white people and usually kept away from their company. She had experienced gender-related racial slurs, which included but was not confined to the word squaw.

Helen had left the boarding home ran by a white family that took in Aboriginal students at about eight o'clock that night. She had a few drinks through the hours, even a few in the back of her home (unknown to the owners) and had squabbled with another Aboriginal girl who had her sights on the same boyfriend and was with him that night. She left sad and a little drunk. The last friend who talked to her, George, who was also from Norway House, parted company with Helen at about 11:30 p.m., as she walked down the infamous Edwards Avenue.

The car bearing the four young white men slowed down to stop beside her. Here was a mudlark for their enjoyment. She was asked whether she wanted to "go to a party"; she said "No." She would know what that request was really about. The car and the men trolled alongside her, trying to persuade her to come join them in the car. She continued to decline the offer. Then Johnston jumped out of the car and pulled the diminutive (a little over five feet) Cree girl into the back seat with himself and Colgan. They would fight inside the car, with Johnston trying to force her to drink, as the others were doing. Crammed in the car between Colgan and Johnston, she was physically and sexually assaulted, as her aggressors ripped open her blouse and grabbed at her breasts. Helen resisted and screamed, until finally, in a secluded spot, some 24 kilometres out of town, they took her to the cabin owned by Houghton's parents. Johnston took her out and beat her, while she swung back, getting in some ineffectual blows.

Worried that her screams of pain and anger would be heard by people who might be in the area, they forced her back into the car and drove to a pump house near a former residential school. Johnston hauled her back outside and began assaulting her again. Johnston somehow managed to take her clothing off as he fought her. The others continued to drink. There were periods of quiet, broken by screaming and by the sounds of a person or persons banging against the side and the rear of the car. Then Johnston came back into the car to fetch a screwdriver. He would stab her over 50 times, breaking her skull, cheekbones, and palate, damaging her lungs and one kidney, bruising her body extensively, and, of course, killing her.

Her face had been smashed so viciously and thoroughly that it was beyond recognition. Thirty-one people, including residents of her home reserve of Norway House, and the man with whom Helen was boarding in The Pas, were unable to identify her body conclusively. It was only after fingerprints had been taken from one of her school books, and these fingerprints were matched with those on her lifeless hands, that a definite identification was finally made.

The First Suspects Were Aboriginal

The day after the murder, Cornelius Bighetty (who graduated from Margaret Barbour Collegiate Institute in 1975) became the first suspect, as his name was tattooed on one of Osborne's legs, in the words "Cornelius Bighetty I love you! No Matter What." He was interrogated, repeatedly told, "I know you did it," and shown flashcards of the mutilated body of his female friend. Frightened of the white police officers and intimidated by the situation, he was uncooperative with the police during interrogation. This lack of cooperation led to his being tossed in jail for a few hours. In Bighetty's words, "They figured I must have something to hide, but I wasn't used to this and I didn't want to talk about it" (Priest, 1989, p. 71).

Afterwards, in what could be considered a remarkable act of forgiveness, or an unconscious acknowledgement of his expectations as an Aboriginal person of how he would be treated by non-Aboriginal police, Bighetty said to the AJI that "he had no complaint about the way he was treated by the police." Still, he did also say that "he would not allow the police to treat his own children the way he was by the RCMP" (www.ajic.mb.ca). Helen's close friend Annaliese Dumas was also treated as a suspect in the case in similar ways. Other Native kids were brought in from school and interrogated, some of them thrown in jail for a while as well for being less than cooperative with the police. Finally, after agreeing to a lie detector test, Bighetty was released. Other Aboriginal teenagers would submit to that test as well.

The Aboriginal Justice Inquiry was critical of the way in which the local police handled this crucial first part of their investigation and remarked on the fact that much of it involved "conscious racism." In their words, "The manner in which the police pursued their initial investigation by rounding up and questioning only Aboriginal students was motivated, at least in part, by racism" (www.ajic.mb.ca).

It should be noted that the police also did not obtain the consent of the parents of the Aboriginal students that they questioned. Nor did the police advise the parents afterwards that official questioning of their children had taken place, treating both Aboriginal parents and their teenage children like second-class citizens. Hamilton reports that in one case, a friend of Helen's was "driven to a lonely country spot and threatened" (Hamilton, 2001, p. 72).

Not having to go through this type of interrogation, the four white culprits still did not seem shy about telling stories about what happened. As such stories do in such places, their tales went "small town viral," with invented details and different degrees of blame being handed out to both killers and victim. Certainly, though the four culprits were well-known, so much so that Aboriginal girls made a point of memorizing what they looked like, so they too would not become victims. They would have to take care of themselves. There was no sense that the town or its police department would see to their defence. In his work for the Aboriginal Justice Inquiry, Judge A. C. Hamilton came to question several policing and general justice practices that had hindered the due process of justice in this case. One relates to the Colgan car, which had been identified by December 1971. It was not thoroughly checked for incriminating evidence. The evidence, including bloodstains, hair, and a tattered brassiere were there, as would be eventually discovered seven months after the murder. Why was the car not investigated earlier? According to Hamilton:

> When the question of bringing the car in for examination arose, an officer from the town detachment said he had checked it, so it was not searched. It turned out that he had only glanced into the back seat...No thorough examination of the car and its contents was made for six or seven months. Mr. Colgan Sr. [the manager of the local Manitoba Liquor Control Commission store] was well known in The Pas and the police seemed to have assumed that as he was a respected citizen, his vehicle could not possibly have been involved. (Hamilton, 2001, p. 68)

The contrast in status between a white middle-class car owner and an Aboriginal female victim would seem to have been a factor here.

How Much Did the Town and the Police Know?

Journalist Lisa Priest entitled her book on the this case *Conspiracy of Silence*, saying in essence that the white people of the town knew, the police knew but conspired to keep quiet. Certainly, the four suspects were not silent about what had been done. At parties, under the influence of alcohol, the story of Helen's murder was told repeatedly. In a trailer camp party in the winter of 1972, a 14-year-old girl heard Dwayne Johnston suddenly say, "I picked up a screwdriver and I stabbed her, and I stabbed her and I stabbed her" (Priest, 1989, p. 96). He even made stabbing motions to illustrate what he was saying.

The police had some idea as well, as they would at local bars order free vodka and orange juice drinks (aka screwdrivers) for Lee Colgan. He was even sent a few screwdrivers in the mail, anonymously, possibly from the police.

Yet nothing serious was done, until an outsider, who, like others before him, was offered the Helen Betty Osborne investigation as a cold case in 1982, and he came to be interested, passionate about the case. His name was Constable Bob Urbanoski of the Thompson, Manitoba detachment of the RCMP. He was twenty-nine years old and only had seven years' experience as a police officer. He submitted a proposal to take the case on in 1983, and it was accepted. By 1984, he was on the case full time. While he initially had no more information than his predecessors on the case, he did obtain the distinct advantage of a large budget, cooperation from the attorney-general's office, the legal right to tap the phones of the suspects, and the accumulated thoughts of officers who had been involved with the case before.

By June 1985, he put in an ad in the local paper, the *Opasquia Times*, that began with the words, "The RCMP are requesting the public's assistance in the investigation of a murder that took place over 13 years ago" (Priest, 1989, p. 122). Interestingly, the ad involved what I would term a distorting flattery by saying that "police have had a terrific response from the public on the case to date." The ad concluded by stating that any information, "No matter how trivial it is," would be useful. Such information began to come in, including the story about Dwayne Johnston and his telling his tale at the trailer camper party. A case was made, charges were issued. Lee Colgan was able to plea bargain to avoid a charge by providing information about the case.

Eliminating the Aboriginal Jurors

One hundred and four prospective jurors were considered for jury duty for the case by the lawyers for the Crown (the prosecution) and for the defence. Of this number, 23 were Aboriginal. The jury would be all non-Aboriginal. Why is that? In part it was because there is the unrealistic but popular notion that, in trials involving Aboriginal people (as victims or as suspects), Aboriginal people will allow their subjective biases to influence their decisions, but non-Aboriginal people will not, that they are somehow, magically, completely objective. One of the lawyers for the defence made his belief in that bias fairly clear: "There was no deliberate campaign to keep the Natives off...But we didn't want these men to be convicted for all of the ills of society" (Priest, 1989, p. 143). The second sentence contradicts the first.

This idea plus a little systemic racism that allowed for the elimination of potential Aboriginal jurors allowed the elimination to happen. There were three constitutionally valid ways of doing this at that time. One was called **standing aside**. This is a way of, without giving any reason, passing on potential jurors until the next round or go-through. They could not go through this twice. This has since been changed. The second way is called **peremptory challenges**, in which the juror can be challenged by the prosecutor or defence, without reason being given. In his discussion of this problem with respect to the Helen Betty Osborne case, one of the commissioners of the AJI, Alvin J. Hamilton, advocated having only **challenge with cause**, where the reason for challenging the potential juror is articulated and the judge gets to decide whether the cause is sufficient to prejudice the case. In assessing the situation, Hamilton stated:

> It is an insult to Aboriginal people to assume they will not discharge their responsibilities as jurors according to law. There should be no assumption that any

> prospective juror "is not indifferent between Her Majesty the Queen and the accused." If counsel[s] are concerned about the independence of a potential juror, they should question the person before they are [i.e., he or she is] sworn-in as a juror and challenge them for cause if they wish. (Hamilton, 2001, p. 70)

Only one of the young men was convicted, Dwayne Johnston. He served a mere 10 years for his crime and was released from prison on full parole in October 1997. There was considerable protest at the time by a number of Aboriginal groups, but to no avail.

The Mandate of the Aboriginal Justice Inquiry

We have referred in the previous chapter to the Aboriginal Justice Inquiry, that was held after the J. J. Harper and the Helen Betty Osborne cases became news. Regarding their treatment of the Helen Betty Osborne case the mandate of the Aboriginal Justice Inquiry (AJI) was

> to have the right to investigate into the death of Helen Betty Osborne and all aspects of the laying and prosecution of charges which followed, including whether the right persons were charged, whether the appropriate charges were laid, whether charges should have been laid earlier, whether immunity from prosecution should have been granted to Lee Colgan, whether there exists any evidence of racial prejudice with respect to the investigation of the death of Helen Betty Osborne, whether the acts or omissions of any persons outside the Police Department impaired the investigation and whether the prosecution was properly conducted. (http://www.majic.mb.ca)

While no specific actions of prosecution or clear blame was attached to the officers involved, the evidence of institutionalized racial prejudice was confirmed.

Acts in Honour of Helen Betty Osborne

On July 14, 2000, a formal apology was given by Gordon MacIntosh, the Minister of Justice of the Manitoba government. It included the following words:

> On behalf of the Government of Manitoba, I wish to express my profound regret at the way the justice system as a whole responded to the death of Betty, and to apologize for the clear lack of justice in her case… The examination of her tragic murder through the Aboriginal Justice Inquiry continues to define the path we are following to ensure justice for all Manitobans. (www.gov.mb.ca/chc/press/top/2000/07/2000-07-14-02.html)

The province also committed $50,000 to create a scholarship in her name, with the yearly scholarships going to female Aboriginal students studying education, and in need of financial assistance.

Another Family Tragedy: The Case of Felicia Solomon

Felicia Solomon, a cousin of Helen Betty Osborne, was born in 1986, the same year that her cousin's case came up. Felicia, like her cousin, was born at Norway House Cree Nation. When she was sixteen and still attending high school while living with her family in Winnipeg, she disappeared on the evening of March 25, 2003. Her mother, who had to go Norway House to attend the funeral of her brother, Felicia's uncle, could not file a missing person report until the morning of March 30. No officers came to her house until 1:00 a.m.; and when they did come, they acted in a way that Felicia's mother believed was disrespectful.

The family arranged to have posters put up, with no assistance from the police, who made no attempt to publicize Felicia's disappearance. A press conference was arranged through the Assembly of Manitoba Chiefs. According to the family, the media made allusions to Felicia being a gang member and a prostitute, based largely on her being Aboriginal, and living in a poor, dangerous area.

Parts of her body, including an arm and a leg were discovered by the Winnipeg Police Service River Patrol in June 2003. Forensic analysis identified the body parts as being those of Felicia Solomon. The case is still unsolved.

The Abuse of Aboriginal Women by Aboriginal Men

It would be misleading and a kind of "whitewash" to say that Aboriginal women such as Helen Betty Osborne are abused only by non-Aboriginal men. They are abused by Aboriginal men as well, not a traditional practice, but a currently prevalent one. Aboriginal male spousal abuse of Aboriginal girls and women has reached what sociologists James Frideres and others have referred to as "epidemic proportions." He sums this up succinctly in the following quotation:

> Aboriginal women [in 2004] report spousal assault at a rate (21 percent) that is three times higher than that for non-Aboriginal women. Research shows that women are, on average, abused 35 times before they leave the relationship and seek help. Aboriginal women only report the most severe and potentially life-threatening forms of violence…and this rate (54 percent) has been consistent over the past decade; yet for non-Aboriginal women, the rate of severe violence has decreased to nearly 35 percent. Overall homicide rates for Aboriginal women are about eight times the rate for non-Aboriginal women. (Frideres, 2012, p. 152)

Table 2.1 was published in *First Nations, Métis and Inuit Women*, published in 2011. This rate of abuse of Aboriginal women affects their abuse by the legal system as well. Aboriginal women are sometimes arrested for how they resist spousal abuse. Made more vulnerable by many of their men, they become more vulnerable to discretionary abuse by the policing system.

One large complication concerning spousal abuse on the reserves is that the conflict is not just between the man and the woman but between their families as well. If a woman accuses a man of spousal abuse on the close-knit, hard-to-escape world of the reserve, she has to deal with his family as well. And his family may include band chiefs, band councillors, or even tribal police if such exist.

Another aspect of this complex situation is that diversion from prison is a growing phenomenon in the way that the

Table 2.1.
Self-reported Spousal Violence for Aboriginal and non-Aboriginal Populations, aged 15 and over (2009)

	Aboriginal Women	Non-Aboriginal Women
Percentage who reported being physically or sexually victimized by a spouse in the previous 5 years	15%	6%
Percentage of those who had been physically or sexually victimized by a spouse in the previous 5 years, reported that they:		
had been sexually assaulted, beaten, choked, or threatened with a knife	48%	32%
sustained an injury	58%	41%
feared for their life	52%	31%

Source: O'Donnell & Wallace (2011, p. 41, table 12)

justice system treats Aboriginal people, one that reflects the cultural traditions of the people. Generally, this can be seen as a good thing. However, a problem arises when the "diverted" potential prisoner has committed spousal abuse and is returned to his reserve community. In the tiny world that is a reserve, reserve-based alternatives to prison can readily put the woman in a dangerous, very threatened position.

The Aboriginal women who speak out in Anne McGillvray and Brenda Comaskey's *Black Eyes All of the Time: Intimate Violence, Aboriginal Women, and the Justice System* (1999), which is based on the authors' analysis of research they initiated with interviews with 26 women in Winnipeg in the summer of 1995, argue that they can only feel safe if those who abused them serve jail time. Otherwise, they might have to leave the reserve and be exposed to the dangers of urban Aboriginal life.

John Martin Crawford: Canada's Least Known Serial Killer

In his 2001 book, *Just Another Indian: a serial killer and Canada's Indifference* long-time journalist Warren D. Goulding, wrote about Canada's least known serial killer, John Martin Crawford. His book not only profiles the murderer and his killings, but it also is critical of the media's lack of reporting of this serial killer.

In 1981, in Lethbridge, Alberta, Crawford, then 19 years old, brutally sexually assaulted, beat, and killed Mary Jane Serloin, a Sarcee from the Calgary area. He received a 10- year sentence for this series of offences but was paroled in September 1987. He went back in five months for violating the conditions of his parole but was out again on March 1989.

His next victim was Shelley Napone, a Cree young woman of 16, whom he drove to a friend of hers, offered her some beer, had sex with her, and killed her. She was killed in 1991, but her body was not discovered until 1994. In that same year, the body of Eva Taysup, the Saulteaux mother of four, was discovered. She had disappeared in 1992. His fourth victim was 22-year-old Calinda Waterhen. He called her parents in January 1992, saying that she was scared and wanted her parents to pick her up from Saskatoon. By the time they got there, it was too late; she had disappeared. Her smothered body would also come to light in 1994.

In 1994, during the four-month period in which he was under police surveillance, Crawford raped and beat another young Aboriginal woman. When they arrived shortly afterwards, they put her in prison overnight, as she was hesitant to press charges against the serial killer. Finally, in 1996, he was convicted of the deaths of Napone, Taysup, and Waterhen killings. It was not nearly as big news as was the Paul Bernardo conviction of the previous year. Bernardo's victims were white.

There are three other similar deaths of which Crawford is merely suspected. He had been charged with raping Janet Sylvestre, another Aboriginal woman, in 1992. The charge was stayed when she failed to show up for court, but he spent a month in jail before his mother put up the $4,000 in bail. Sylvestre disappeared, to be seen again as a corpse in 1994. By 2001, the police still had not found her killer. Crawford had both motive and opportunity. The two other victims were Shirley Lonethunder (see below) and Cynthia Baldhead.

Goulding is quick to spot the bias of the press and the ways in which they appear to be blaming the victim. The following is an example:

> This injustice manifests itself in biased portrayals of women such as Eva, Calinda, and Shelley. Journalists seek out juicy quotes that carry sinister, unspoken messages. "Sometimes she would bring strangers home from the bar," was one such revelation. You can almost hear the tongues clucking and the heads shaking as readers absorb such comments. Was Eva Taysup the first young woman to bring a man home from a bar? Of course not. It occurs regularly in all sectors of society. But by exposing the imperfections in their lifestyles, the media assassinate the characters of the victims, rarely finding the positive aspects that are there if only they took the time to search for them. (Goulding, 2001, pp. 213-214)

Shirley Lonethunder

One of the three women that Crawford is merely suspected of killing is Shirley Lonethunder, a Cree mother of two who disappeared sometime late in 1991. She was 25 years old at that time and planning to go to university. In March 1992, her mother, Doris Lonethunder, who had been taking care of Shirley's children to enable her to start university in the new year, filed a missing person report with the Saskatoon Police Service. The Amnesty International website that tells her story wrote the following about the police reaction her disappearance:

> The Saskatoon Police Service's missing persons policy states that investigators have a responsibility to

"liaise with complainants" and should request media assistance, if necessary, to help locate a missing person. According to Doris Lonethunder, the police investigator was in regular contact with her at first, phoning every week for approximately a month, and then phoning every two weeks. However, the police did not make any public appeals for assistance on the case and the family members felt the police were not very supportive. After about three months, the investigator stopped phoning. Approximately six months after having filed a Missing Person report, Shirley Lonethunder's brother contacted the Saskatoon Police to enquire about any progress in the case. He says that he was told there was no record of the Missing Person report. (www.amnesty.ca/campaigns/sisters_shirley-lonethunder.php)

The Highway of Tears

The 720-kilometre-long stretch of Highway 16 in northern British Columbia, joining the cities of Prince George and Prince Rupert is known as the "Highway of Tears" in the area, and more recently nationally. This is because a number of young women, almost all of them Aboriginal, have been murdered or gone missing there. The following women are those commonly identified as victims of the Highway of Tears:

1970 – Micheline Pare (18)
1989 – Alberta Williams (24)
1989 – Cecilia Anne Nikal (?)
1990 – Delphine Nikkal (16)
1994 – Ramona Wilson (16)
     – Roxanne Thiara (15)
     – Alishia Germaine (15)
1995 – Lana Derrick (19)
2002 – Nicole Hoar (25)
2005 – Tamara Chipman (22)
2006 – AieLah Auger (14)

On September 25, 2012, an announcement was made by officials from Project E-PANA, an RCMP initiative named after an Inuit goddess in charge of the recently dead, a task force that began in the fall of 2005. The goal of this task force was "to determine if a serial killer, or killers, is responsible for murdering young women traveling along major highways in BC (www.highwayoftears.ca). They investigated 18 murders or disappearances, not just on Highway 16, but in other highways in the area as well.

A DNA analysis related to one particular case in 1974 was undertaken in 2007, with no matches with known suspects. In 2012, with the improvement of DNA techniques, the analysis qualified to be sent to INTERPOL. A match was found with US citizen, Bobby Jack Fowler, who had died in 2006 after serving 10 years for a violent attack on a woman in Oregon. He had a history of casual employment in British Columbia. He is still a person of interest with respect to some of the killings of women in the area, but the murders of most of the Aboriginal women still remain unsolved.

The Robert Pickton Case

The case of Robert William "Willie" Pickton, Port Coquitlam pig farmer is perhaps Canada's most spectacular case of serial killing. He was arrested in 2002 and convicted in 2007 of the second-degree murders of six women. While he was charged with 20 more murders, these charges were stayed on August 4, 2010. The slowness and reluctance with which the murders were dealt with by the Vancouver police ably illustrates the idea that some women are considered disposable people, persons that the police, social agencies, and the media show little interest in. They were sex-trade workers, many of them; they lived in the notorious and neglected neighbourhood of Downtown Eastside Vancouver. Many were hooked on drugs. And, of course, most were Aboriginal. The combination made for perfect victims if you want your killing to be under-investigated. As one police officer, "The problem was that there was always a feeling within the organization [the Vancouver Police Department] that 'hypes' [prostitutes who sell sex to make enough money for their drugs] and whores are disposable" (as cited in Cameron, 2010, p. 213). This idea that the victims were disposable made the force less interested in pursuing the women's disappearances with the effort required to solve the crimes before more and more victims were added to the list.

The mainstream media, which during the trial presented the gory findings at length, never really focused on the Aboriginal identity of many of the victims. The exception is a 2006 documentary, *Finding Dawn*, produced by Métis filmmaker and university professor Christine Welsh. The central subject of the documentary was Dawn Teresa Crey who was killed at 43, although the film also dealt with the Highway of Tears victim Ramona Wilson.

Recent Efforts to Draw Attention to the Dangerous Situation of Aboriginal Women

The continuing profoundly negative experience of Aboriginal women, their interlocking matrix or intersectionality of oppression, can be seen in the growing number of websites about such women that have been murdered or are missing. Amnesty International Canada's website, *No More Stolen Sisters*, includes comments that illustrate the interlocking matrix of oppression of Aboriginal women:

> "There's still a double standard when it comes to Aboriginal women and girls. When is the government going to take action to make sure that every case of missing and murdered Aboriginal women and girls is thoroughly investigated?"
> –Laurie Odjick (whose 16-year-old daughter disappeared in September 2008)

> "Refusing to keep track of the numbers of our sisters and daughters who have been murdered or gone missing is just another way of ignoring the trouble."
> –Gwenda Yuzippi (whose 19-year-old daughter was murdered)
> *Amnesty International, No More Stolen Sisters.*)

In 2004, Amnesty International in Canada published *Stolen Sisters: A Human Rights Response to Discrimination and Violence Amongst Indigenous Women in Canada*. It began with a short telling of Helen Betty Osborne's story and led to others distressingly similar. Other websites often start with her story.

The problem has yet to go away. In recognition of the simple fact that Aboriginal women represent a serious at-risk group for being murdered or missing, in 2005, the Sisters in Spirit Initiative, a joint effort of the federal government and the Native Women's Association of Canada (a coordinated network of smaller Native Women's Associations), began. There was a felt need of draw attention to the problem and to initiate action to lessen the problem. Five year's funding produced, among other gains, in 2010 the important publication, *What Their Stories Tell Us: Research Findings from the Sisters in Spirit Initiative.* Among their research findings were the following:

> (1) Between 2000 and 2008, there were 153 cases of murdered Aboriginal women in Canada, representing 10 percent of homicides of women, an over-representation. I should note that this number will be less than the actual figure. The Pickton case alone has yet to determine how many Aboriginal women were killed and deposited in his British Columbia pig farm.
>
> (2) Some 115 Aboriginal women were still missing.
>
> (3) Most of the murdered and missing were young, under 31 years of age (2010, p.10).

On December 13, 2011, the United Nations Committee on the Elimination of Discrimination against Women reported that, after what it felt was inadequate response to earlier questions concerning this situation, it had decided to conduct an inquiry into the murders and disappearances of Aboriginal women and girls across Canada. The committee is composed of 23 independent experts from around the world and is the UN's main authority on women's human rights.

Conclusions

We have seen in this chapter that Aboriginal women murder victims such as Helen Betty Osborne and the victims of serial killer John Martin Crawford have not had their cases treated with respect by the Canadian justice system. This is seen in a number of ways. The lax prosecution of the perpetrators, the failure to adequately make public young Aboriginal women who have disappeared, and whose families have filed missing person reports, all are contributing factors. The stereotype of the perpetually sexually available and generally immoral squaw has had an impact on that lack of respect. There is a definite need for change here, new structures, new strategies, and a systematic taking apart of the squaw stereotype. All are needed.

Questions

1. Is there anything you would have added to the mandate of the Aboriginal Justice Inquiry with respect to the Helen Betty Osborne case?

2. How different a reaction do you think there would have been if the Helen Betty Osborne's murder had been of a girl who was a white high school student?

3. Why do you think that it took so long for a trial to occur in her case?

4. How do you insure that potential suspects and witnesses that are Aboriginal and non-Aboriginal receive the same treatment?

5. The report of the Aboriginal Justice Inquiry questioned why the suspects, who were well-known to be suspects at least by 1972, were not brought into the station and questioned, which is a well-established policing practice that was certainly applied with respect to Aboriginal people thought to possibly have knowledge about the case. They suggested that the middle-class status of at least two of the suspects was a factor. Why do you think these suspects were not brought down to the station for questioning?

6. One method of dealing with the negative stereotype of the "squaw" is to eliminate the word from place names (e.g., Squaw Valley) in the United States and Canada. Do you think that this will have any effect? How would you act to diminish the influence of the stereotype of the squaw?

7. How might the situation of the Highway of Tears be best handled? Is there an efficient method of policing this isolated highway?

8. Do you think that the 20 additional cases relating to Robert Pickton would have been stayed if all of the victims were white?

9. Why do you think that the police responded to the missing person reports in the Pickton murders in the way that they did?
10. What could the police have done that they did not do with respect to the Pickton murders?
11. Why do you think that public notification of a missing Aboriginal person is much less likely than of a non-Aboriginal person?
12. Do you think that there should be a special branch of the RCMP and provincial police forces to deal with missing Aboriginal women? Explain why such should or should not exist.

Key Terms

Bill-C-31–a bill enacted in 1985 changing the Indian Act so that, among other things, status Aboriginal women would not lose their status by marrying non-Aboriginal men, and seeing that some of the descendants of such women would regain their status.

challenge with cause–a challenge of a potential juror by a lawyer that involves stating the specific reason why the challenge has been issued.

desegregation–formal attempt to reduce or eliminate the separation of two racialized groups.

disposable people – people who are considered to be less important, less worthy of justice or fair treatment than other people.

gendering–through legal means and through general practices changing the gender roles and rules in a particular group (in this case Aboriginal people) to more closely match those in another (i.e., in this case that of mainstream Canadian society in the nineteenth century).

Highway of Tears–a highway in northern British Columbia around which a significant number of women, almost all of them Aboriginal, have been murdered or have disappeared.

Indian Act–a federal document first introduced in 1876 that governs the legal relationship between federal governments and Aboriginal people in Canada.

intersecting oppression–the forms of oppression that occur when more than one negatively valued social status (e.g., race, gender, or class) is possessed by an individual.

matrilineal–determining primary family membership on the female or mother's side.

peremptory challenge – a challenge issued by a lawyer concerning a particular potential juror. No cause needs to be presented for this challenge.

racialized space–territory, including neighbourhoods, and "the street" at night, assumed to belong to a particular racialized group.

squaw–the negative stereotype of Aboriginal women that portrays them as of little value except for their sexual exploitation and abuse by male oppressors, Aboriginal and non-Aboriginal.

standing aside – a setting aside of potential jurors for a second round of choosing.

status Indian – someone who according to the federal Indian Act is considered legally an Indian.

References

Aboriginal Justice Implementation Commission. Retrieved from https://www.ajic.mb.ca/volumeII/chapter 5.html

Acoose, J. (1995). *Iskwewak-Kah' Ki Yaw Ni Wahkomakanak: Neither Indian princess nor easy squaws*, Toronto: Women's Press.

Amnesty International, Canada. (2004). *Stolen sisters: A human rights response to discrimination and violence amongst Indigenous women in Canada.* Retrieved from https://www.amnesty.ca/stolensisters/amr2000304.pdf

Amnesty International, No More Stolen Sisters. Retrieved from www.amnesty.ca

Black Coffee Poet (2011). Breaking the silence about canada's 800+ missing and murdered Aboriginal women: Interview with Cree academic and activist Robyn Bourgeois + a photo essay of the "no more silence" rally Feb 14th 2011 (Toronto). Retrieved from http://blackcoffeepoet.com

Cameron, S. (2010). *On the farm: Robert William Pickton and the tragic story of Vancouver's missing women.* Toronto: Knopf Canada.

Comack, E. (2012). *Racialized policing: Aboriginal People's encounters with the police.* Halifax: Fernwood Publishing.

Cummins, B.D., & Steckley, J.L. (2003). *Aboriginal policing: A Canadian perspective.* Toronto: Pearson Canada.

Frideres, J.S., & Gadacz, R.R. (2012). *Aboriginal Peoples in Canada* (9th ed.). Toronto: Pearson Canada.

Goulding, W.D. (2001). *Just another Indian: A serial killer and Canada's indifference.* Markham, ON: Fifth House.

Hamilton, A.C. (2001). *A feather not a gavel: Working towards Aboriginal justice.* Winnipeg: MB: Great Plains Publications.

Hearne, S. (1958). *A journey to the Northern Ocean.* Edited by Richard Glover. Toronto, ON: The Macmillan Company.

Klein, L.F., & Ackerman, L.A. (1995). "Introduction." In L.F Klein & L.A. Ackerman (Eds.), *Women and power in Native North America* (pp. 3-16). Norman, OK: University of Oklahoma Press.

McGillvray, A., & Comaskey, B. (1999). *Black eyes all of the time: Intimate violence, Aboriginal women, and the justice system.* Toronto, ON: University of Toronto Press.

O'Donnell, V., & Wallace, S. (2011). First Nations, Métis and Inuit women. In Women in Canada: A gender-based statistical report. Ottawa, ON: Social and Aboriginal Statistics Division, Statistics Canada.

Native Women's Association of Canada. (2010). *What their stories tell us: Research findings from the Sisters in Spirit initiative.* Retrieved from www.nwac.ca

Manitoba Government, New Release. (2000, July 14). Helen Betty Osborne. Scholarship fund established. Apology to family. Legislation to Honor Osborne. Retrieved from www.gov.mb.ca/chc/press/top/2000/07/2000-07-14-02.html

Priest, L. (1989). *A Conspiracy of silence.* Toronto, ON: McClelland & Stewart.

Rhodes, R.A. (1985). *Eastern Ojibwa-Chippewa-Ottawa dictionary.* Berlin: Mouton de Gruyter.

Robertson, H. (1970). *Reservations are for Indians.* Toronto, ON: James Lorimer.

Smith, Debi. (2006, February, 28). Our highway of tears. *Hiway 16 Magazine.* Retreived from http://www.bc-north.ca/magazine/pages/Debi/tears/tears1.htm

Steckley, J. (1999). *Beyond their years: Five Native Women's stories.* Toronto, ON: Canadian Scholars' Press.

Steckley, J., & Cummins, B. (2008). *Full circle: Canada's First Nations* (2nd ed.). Toronto, ON: Pearson Canada.

Welsh, C. (2006). *Finding Dawn.* Documentary film. National Film Board.

Chapter 3

The Donald Marshall Jr. Case

Introduction

In assessing the police and general justice system in their handling of the Donald Marshall Jr. case, the commissioners of the Royal Commission on the Donald Marshall, Jr. Prosecution concluded:

> The criminal justice system failed Donald Marshall, Jr. at virtually every turn from his arrest and wrongful conviction for murder in 1971 up to, and even beyond his acquittal by the Court of Appeal in 1983. The tragedy of the failure is compounded by evidence that this miscarriage of justice could–and should–have been prevented, or at least corrected quickly, if those involved in the system had carried out their duties in a professional and/or competent manner. That they did not is due, in part at least, to the fact that Donald Marshall Jr. is a Native. (Hickman, Poitras, & Evans, 1989, p. 1)

RCMP investigator, Harry Wheaton, commented on the cavalier attitude of the attorney general of Nova Scotia concerning the Marshall case around the time of the successful appeal. The official came to their annual dinner. Wheaton stated that the attorney general

> didn't understand why the press was making all the fuss over the Marshall case. I had to be restrained from leaving the room in the middle of his speech. The man simply didn't realize the suffering and

heartache involved in this thing, nor the immense social issues that are still at play. I just couldn't stomach
the trivializing of a case that changed so many people's lives and my whole outlook as a policeman.
(Harris, 1991, pp. 402-403)

The wrongful conviction and imprisonment of Donald
Marshall Jr., a Mi'kmaq from the northern Cape Breton area
of Nova Scotia, was an important catalyst in changing Nova
Scotia's legal system to one that participated less in systemic
racism and more in greater justice. The Marshall Inquiry gen-
erated some specific recommendations that changed the face
of justice in the province. Whether that change will prevent a
similar occurrence in the future is still open to question.

Background

The Mi'kmaq (formerly spelled Micmac) people of
Canada have communities in all four Atlantic provinces and
in Quebec. There are more than 20,000 "registered Indians"
that are Mi'kmaq. Thirteen Mi'kmaq communities exist in
Nova Scotia. The people were longer involved with the European settler groups than any other Aboriginal group in
Canada, associating in particular with the French, including
the Acadians. They have survived stronger than similar east
coast people in the United States, some of which disappeared
as distinct groups. The Mi'kmaq fought against the English
for decades during the eighteenth century but still managed
to stay intact. Their language (often now referred to as Mi'k-
maw) has added two words to commonly used Canadian English: Quebec (meaning "it narrows," referring to the St.
Lawrence River as it narrows around Isle d'Orleans beside the
city of Quebec); and "caribou" (said to mean "it scratches,"
referring to how the animal obtains food in the winter, scratch-
ing through the snow). The Mi'kmaq speak an Algonquian
(not Algonquin, which is an Algonquian language), closely
related to languages such as Maliseet (who live in New
Brunswick), Abenaki (who live in Quebec), and Delaware
(who live in southwestern Ontario) more distantly connected
with Innu, Cree, and Ojibwe, and farther, yet from the languages of the Blackfeet Confederacy (the Siksika or Black-

foot, Kainai or Blood, and the Piegan) of Alberta. There were traditionally seven districts of the Mi'kmaq people, one of which was Cape Breton, where this case took place.

Membertou First Nation

The Membertou First Nation (named after the first baptized Mi'kmaq, Henri Membertou who lived during the sixteenth and early seventeenth centuries), where Donald Marshall Jr. was born and raised is what can be called an "urban reserve." The main reserve is located in an area between the two main sections of Sydney, Nova Scotia,[1] near the northern tip of Cape Breton in Nova Scotia. The community did not always live at that location, but a petition drawn up by white people in the area in 1915 led to the removal of the 125 Mi'kmaq who lived on King's Road in what is now Sydney. It was decided that the presence of the Mi'kmaq there would impede progress and depress property values. The people of the community were forcibly scattered to other reserves until, in 1925, the federal government bought the land where the present main reserve now is found.

As of October 2012, Membertou First Nation has a population of 1,352, with 824 living on one of their reserves. The community is financially in a relatively good position; part of that position owes to fact that, since the mid-1990s, there has been a gaming site and the Membertou Trade and Convention Centre located there (the latter costing $7.2 million and seating 900 people), and the chief and council have established a very corporate and successful financial plan that has succeeded where others have failed. When Donald Marshall Jr. was a boy, however, it was not nearly so well off, and children were heavily involved with substance abuse, which involved glue and gas sniffing, as well as drinking vanilla and shaving lotion and other substances for the alcohol they contain.

Racializing Clemency: Executing Indians First and Foremost

When killers were still executed in Canada, Aboriginal people were those most likely to face the proverbial hangman's noose (hanging was the only method ever used in

Canada for execution). Kenneth L. Avio, an economist who teaches as the University of Victoria and specializes in justice issues, studied how often executive clemency or the "royal prerogative," the Canadian version of the American governor's pardon, was used during the years 1926 to 1957; he found that Aboriginal people were the ones most likely to be left to their deadly fate. During this time, 440 killers were convicted, 72% of them executed. Regarding the race issue, if an Aboriginal person killed another Aboriginal person, the risk of execution was 62% (a **racial devaluing of the victim**). If the victim were white, however, the chance of the convicted Aboriginal person being executed was 96%, a **racial devaluing of the killer**. If the killer were white, then risk was only 21%. Avio found that one key factor in this pattern was the attitude of the Department of Indian Affairs. He discovered a significant number of memos encouraging the death penalty for Natives as they required a "special deterrence" against killing people (Avio 1987). The last person executed in Canada was in 1962, although execution was still possible until 1976. It is a good thing for Donald Marshall that he wasn't convicted of killing a white man, and that public opinion at the time of his conviction was against hanging.

More Statistics

In Nova Scotia, like elsewhere in Canada, Aboriginal people comprise a disproportionately high percentage of the prison population. This is especially true in the Cape Breton region, as can be seen in Table 3.1.

In the Canadian census of 2006, it was recorded that there were 24,175 people claiming Aboriginal status in the province of Nova Scotia, representing roughly 2.7% of the total population.

Donald Marshall Jr.

Donald Marshall Jr. (1953-2009), "Junior" as he was often called, came from a relatively good home. Both his parents worked, which was unusual in his community at that time. His father was a plasterer; his mother was a cleaning lady in a local hospital. Donald Marshall Sr. (1925–1991), his father,

Table 3.1.
Admissions to Adult Custody
by Admission Status and Ethnicity
2004-2005 and 2005-2006

Nova Scotia Corrections

	Period			
	2004-2005		2005-2006	
Race	Remand	Sentence	Remand	Sentence
Caucasian	972 (74%)	1159 (81%)	905 (73%)	1095 (76%)
Black	168 (13%)	119 (8%)	154 (13%)	184 (13%)
Aboriginal	92 (7%)	92 (6%)	95 (8%)	101 (7%)
Other	44 (3%)	27 (2%)	31 (3%)	23 (2%)
Unknown	35 (3%)	40 (3%)	51 (4%)	34 (2%)

Cape Breton Correctional Centre

Caucasian	203 (75%)	258 (82%)	202 (77%)	213 (76%)
Black	7 (3%)	10 (3%)	11 (4%)	9 (3%)
Aboriginal	54 (20%)	44 (14%)	47 (18%)	59 (21%)
Other	4 (2%)	2 (1%)	1 (1%)	0 (0%)
Unknown	3 (1%)	0 (0%)	0 (0%)	1 (1%)

Source: Clairmont & McMillan (2006, p. 40).

was also band chief, as well as being the grand chief ("kji'saq-maw") of the entire Mi'kmaq people, a post he held for 27 years. Junior, as the eldest son, was in a position to inherit that prestigious (but non-salaried) position. He was a somebody in Membertou. But in Sydney, Nova Scotia, he was just a Mi'kmaq, an "Indian."

Marshall had a "history" with the law, which brought him into direct conflict with big (six feet tall, 260 pound) John MacIntyre, sergeant of detectives. In one incident, a group of often trouble- and excitement-seeking Mi'kmaq youths that Marshall hung out with, the "Shipyard Gang," had pushed over the headstone of a MacIntyre grave. Junior was there. MacIntyre told Junior that two of his friends had ratted on him. At the same time, he told his two friends that Junior had been the snitch. Neither statement was true. Trying to trick a suspect with an untruth was a technique to get a conviction. It didn't work this time. It would work later on in a more important case.

Marshall got arrested for supplying alcohol to a minor, including his own girlfriend, and spent four months in county jail, beginning on November 17, 1970. Shortly after getting out, at 17, he was fined $10 for drinking in a public place. A little more than a month later, he and three others were picked up for kicking down a rickety porch late one night. He was not convicted that time; one of his friends took the rap for this offense. But his time was coming soon.

The Murder of Sandy Seale

On the night of May 28, 1971 (the same year as the murder of Helen Betty Osborne), 16-year-old Donald Marshall Jr. encountered someone he knew slightly, a 17-year-old black teenager named Sandy Seale. It should be noted that Seale came from a respectable, middle-class black family, and he did not have a police record. Around midnight, the two teenage boys decided to go walking through Wentworth Park, a common hangout at night for Sydney's youth. There they spotted two white men in the park, Roy Ebsary, 59, and Jimmy MacNeil, 25, who had been drinking heavily (reportedly seven beers each). The teenagers decided to see if they could ask the drunk white men for some money. It seems that panhandling was not unusual in that park, which was a somewhat dangerous place at night sometimes. The four talked for a while. Ebsary even asked them over to his place for some drinks. The teenagers hinted with increasing forcefulness that they would appreciate a little money. Things became a little more aggressive. Marshall and MacNeil began to wrestle with and push each other. Seale, standing right in front of the older white man, asked Ebsary to empty out his pockets. What he did not know was that Ebsary had been mugged for money several times in that park and was ready to strike out at the next person who asked him for money. He also did not know, until it was too late, that Ebsary was carrying a very large knife and was prepared to use it. Ebsary responded to Seale's request with a swift and powerful stab that entered Seale's stomach and came out his back. He lifted him up with the blow. When Marshall saw this, he moved towards the old man, only to be cut by a slashing motion of the knife. Marshall, Ebsary and MacNeil all ran from the scene of the crime. The two white men went to Ebsary's place. His 13-year-old daughter Donna saw her father washing blood off of his knife later that night, something she would not reveal until much later. Seale would die of his wounds in less than a day.

There were no eye witnesses to the murder other than those surviving three who had been directly involved. However, several others would become involved in the aftermath of the killing and would eventually be converted into witnesses by the police. One of those converted witnesses was Maynard Chant, who was 14 at the time. As his night out was ending, he planned to take a shortcut through the park so he could hitchhike home. He ran into Marshall, who showed him a gash about 10 cm long on his arm that was bleeding profusely. Marshall told the younger boy that two men in the park had cut him and that his friend was lying in the park with a knife in his stomach. Marshall would tell that same true story to several others that he encountered that night.

The police were called by an ex-RCMP officer who heard the teenagers talking outside the window of his house. When the first police vehicle appeared on the scene, they were flagged down by Marshall. He showed them his bloody arm and said that he and his friend had been attacked with a knife, after which he described their assailants: a young white man and an older shorter white man in a coat like that of a priest. After a brief discussion, one of the officers took Marshall to the hospital to have his arm stitched up, after which he was told that he could go home. The police drove him back to the reserve. Seale arrived at the same hospital by ambulance. He would not return home. Maynard Chant was interviewed by the police, but as he said that he did not actually witness the crime it was felt that his account was of relatively minor importance. He was allowed to go home.

The Investigation

MacIntyre took over the investigation, with no solid leads to guide him with the case. Marshall quickly became the prime suspect. Being "known to the police" (to MacIntyre in particular) and being Native were two strikes against him. He spent a lot of time during the next few days in the police station at MacIntyre's request. The sergeant of detectives also went to Chant's house. He told Chant's parents that he believed that their son had lied to the police during the interview, that the young man should speak to the police again. This time Chant added to the story, filling it with hearsay content. He said that he had actually witnessed the stabbing, that the story followed the outline that Marshall had given him. This was not what MacIntyre wanted to hear. He would be back.

Another non-witness would also become a part of MacIntyre's plan to gain evidence. His name was John Pratico. He was a white teenager, 16, who was allowed to hang out with the Shipyard Gang, more of a hanger-on than a real member. He had been drinking in the park during the night of the murder, but he did not know about what had taken place until he heard about it on the radio. Marshall would later tell him the story of the killing when Pratico was at the reserve.

MacIntyre, perhaps knowing Pratico's membership in the gang, came to his house and asked him what he knew about the murder. Pratico told him the truth, saying that he knew nothing about it but what he had heard later on. But MacIntyre believed that the young man could become a witness if he tried hard enough. In Pratico's words: "He said if you don't tell us about it we're going to put you in jail until you do tell us" (Harris, 1991, p. 64). Eager to respond and not wanting to spend time in jail, he made up imaginary assailants that did not look anything like Ebsary or MacNeil.

There were also people who could have proven useful to Marshall's case with their testimony. On Monday, May 30, two teenagers, George and Roderick (Sandy) McNeil, showed up at the police station in response to the call for witnesses. They had seen Marshall and Seale trying to bum smokes off of a young couple and felt that that information might be important. Their statements were taken, and, unknown to them, corroborated Marshall's story. They were not called back to the trial, as MacIntyre claimed that their evidence was not as important as the statements he had obtained from Chant and Pratico.

The Biggest Lie: A (Manufactured) Break in the Case

The break in the case against Donald Marshall Jr. came when MacIntyre interviewed John Pratico for a second time. Both Harris, in his excellent account of the case, and the commissioners in their inquiry point out that this young man was very emotionally unstable and likely to fantasize when reality did not satisfy. Two months after he gave evidence, he would suffer from a "nervous breakdown" and be placed in a mental institution. It would appear that MacIntyre played to this unstable nature in his approach to Pratico. If they were in court, a judge would have referred to what would take place as "leading the witness." Pratico was led into saying what he "must have seen," repeating a scenario that MacIntyre suggested to him. And he reported that he heard Seale and Marshall having a loud argument, then saw Marshall stab his friend.

Armed with this story, MacIntyre went back to Maynard Chant saying that the police had "evidence" that he had lied, and informed him of the penalty for perjury. MacIntyre and his colleagues pressured the young man, also saying that the other "witness" had seen him there (he hadn't, of course), so his story needed to be different from his first version, the same as the story told by the other witness. The Royal Commission would conclude that "MacIntyre's interview with Maynard Chant was conducted in an intimidating and unacceptable manner" (1989, p. 19).

There was an interesting flaw in the two "witness" statements that was not pursued by the defence at the trial. Both witnesses claimed to be standing on the same stretch of railroad track when they saw Marshall stab Seale, and yet they did not claim to have seen each other. Armed with two alleged corroborations of the same false story, MacIntyre felt that he could now arrest Marshall, which he did on June 4. The trap was almost completely set.

A Third Witness and a Third Changed Story

Fourteen-year-old Patricia Harris was the third "manufactured witness." She and her 20-year-old boyfriend had briefly met with Marshall, with her boyfriend asking for a light for his cigarette. The first three times she spoke with police, the last time at the Sydney police station, Harris described two men that were standing nearby, one of which was clearly Ebsary from the description of a short, old white man with a long dark coat. This was not what MacIntyre wanted to hear. So when he and a colleague came to interview her for a fourth time, more of an interrogation than the previous instances, they got her to change her story so that she said that she had seen Sandy Seale with Marshall. In the words of author Michael Harris,

> During the interrogation, Harris felt that the police were telling her what she should have seen, banging their fists on the table when they were unhappy with what she told them, and changing her statements repeatedly. Finally she, like John Pratico and Maynard Chant, signed a second, and false, statement. Both police officers would later swear that they at no time pressured Harris into implicating Junior Marshall in the Seale murder. (Harris, 1986, p. 92)

With the manipulated stories of two 14-year-olds and one 16-year-old, MacIntyre was ready for legal action.

The Trial

Although MacIntyre actively sought out physical evidence to support his allegation, none was found. In the trial that followed that November 2, the prosecutor, violating the ethics but not the letter of the law of his profession, refused to let the defence see the original versions of the teenagers' testimony. Long after the verdict was delivered, and as a direct result of this case, this strategy would be made illegal in Nova Scotia. Marshall was convicted of murder by a jury of 12 white men (it is not apparent whether there were any Aboriginal potential jurors), taking only four hours (a relatively short time) in their deliberation. On November 5, 1971, the judge sentenced Donald Marshall Jr. to life imprisonment.

Jimmy MacNeil, who had been Ebsary's companion on the night of the stabbing, felt bad about the conviction and the sentence. He did not act because he was threatened by Ebsary's son not to talk and because he did not think that the charge would stick, as he knew that Marshall had not stabbed Seale. Shortly after the verdict was declared, MacNeil told his brother John about what he had witnessed. After talking it over with his family, 10 days after the verdict, Jimmy MacNeil went to the Sydney police to tell them that they had convicted an innocent man, that Ebsary had committed the act. His description of the killing matched the one that Marshall had given during the trial. He added the fact of Ebsary washing off his knife to the story. As MacNeil told his story, MacIntyre tried hard to find lies or misinformation that would show that the story was false, but found no such weaknesses.

The police, led by MacIntyre, went to Ebsary's place to question him and his family. They appear not to have asked about whether he carried a knife, just as they seem not to have checked whether Ebsary had a prior history of violence with knives. Less than a year before the Seale stabbing, he had been charged with carrying an offensive weapon, not surprisingly, a large knife. When MacIntyre questioned Ebsary himself, he accepted his protestations of innocence as truth, feeling that it held more truth than Jimmy MacNeil's contradictory story.

This part of the investigation was passed over to the RCMP by MacIntyre. After listening to MacNeil's story, they concluded simply that the part of the story that detailed stabbing by Ebsary was just a "figment of his imagination" (Harris, 1991 pp. 234-235), so did no further questioning in this line of inquiry. They had no evidence, nor professional corroboration of this quick diagnosis of MacNeil's capacity to imagine (something they would have had of John Pratico, the "witness"). Furthermore, information concerning the new evidence, and the RCMP-run reinvestigation involved was never sent to Marshall's lawyer, as it should have been. It would have given fairly solid grounds for initiating an appeal.

Further evidence would come out in 1974. Now 16, Donna Ebsary informed her martial arts instructor that she had seen her father wash off the knife on the night of the murder. He convinced her to take her story to the police. When the two of them went and told the story, they were told simply that the case was closed. The instructor had a friend in the RCMP and asked him to inquire. He was told it was outside his jurisdiction.

In 1976, Marshall, who was then in a minimum security institution was told that his grandmother had died, and he was given an application for temporary leave of absence to travel back home for the funeral. MacIntyre, who had recently been made the chief of the Sydney police, vetoed the application, saying that he did not want the young man harassing the "witnesses" who testified against him.

In September 1979, when Marshall was 26, he was granted a parole to attend an outdoor survival course. Marshall escaped when he was returning back to prison with a prison guard and two other inmates. He felt that he would never be released so he had little to lose. His freedom was short, as he was picked up by the police at his girlfriend's place. His mother had given them the address.

On the afternoon of August 26, 1981, Marshall was visited by his girlfriend. She had brought her brother Mitchell Sarson with her. He had lived at Roy Ebsary's house when he was attending school in Sydney. Ebsary had bragged to him about "killing a black guy" and "stabbing an Indian." Sarson told Marshall the story. After the visit, Marshall contacted his lawyer, who contacted Daniel Paul of the Union of Nova Scotia Indians. He went to the Sydney police station with the news. The case was reopened. Marshall applied for a day parole to talk his case over with his lawyer and members of the Union of Nova Scotia, but through chief of police MacIntyre, it was denied. There was good news that would shortly follow that bad news. Ebsary had just been charged with knifing someone. MacIntyre passed the case over to the RCMP, again.

They spoke with the three key witnesses. Maynard Chant, after a brief career as a drug pusher, had become a fundamentalist Christian, and believed that telling the truth was best, so he told the new investigators how, contrary to his signed statement, he had never witnessed the stabbing. The other two manufactured witnesses would follow suit, telling of how they had been manipulated into making witnessing statements.

The case went to the Nova Scotia Court of Appeal in the spring of 1982. The Crown prosecutor, rather than dealing directly with the murder, spent much of his time and effort in trying to get Marshall to admit to trying to rob the Ebsary and

MacNeil, even to asking whether he had ever robbed anyone before, which, again, had little to do with the reason for the appeal hearing. While the Crown prosecutor acknowledged that Marshall should be acquitted, he also asked the five judges involved to exonerate the criminal justice system of any blame on the grounds that its reputation must be upheld:

> Here, if the Court does ultimately decide to acquit the Appellant, it is no overstatement to say that the credibility of our criminal justice system may be called into question by a significant portion of the community. It seems reasonable to assume that the public will suspect that there is something wrong with the system if a man can be convicted of a murder he did not commit. A minimum level of public confidence in the criminal justice system must be maintained or it simply will not work. (Harris, 1991, pp. 365-366)

It would have been better that confidence in the system came from its capacity to correct its mistakes, however late that correction may come, and to change its nature so that similar failings not be repeated, but that was not on the Crown prosecutor's mind.

He then proceeded to have Marshall take the blame for the injustice that had struck down 11 years of his life. The words are hard to believe, but here they are:

> To function, our system depends on getting the truth and that is exactly what it did not get in 1971...It is submitted that had the Appellant been forthright [i.e., admitted to trying to commit a robbery], the odds are that both the police investigation and/or his defence would have taken different directions. The likelihood is that he would never have been charged, let alone convicted. (Harris, 1991, p. 366)

He considered Pratico, Chant, and Harris as merely adding to this lack of truth, disregarding that their testimonies were the heart and soul of what convicted Marshall.

The judges accepted this position and blamed Marshall (a classic case of blame the victim for his victimization) more than the system for the lack of justice he received. They felt that he had initiated the series of actions that had led to his conviction and that he had been "evasive" in his answers during the trial, committing perjury in so doing. They also intimated, without evidence, that the killing was initiated by a non-existent "robbery" on his part that the Crown prosecutor was trying to get Marshall to admit to, a robbery for which he had never been charged.

Fortunately, the matter did not end there. Through a Royal Commission, a two-year study followed, revealing anti-Mi'kmaq prejudice deeply embedded in every aspect of the justice system.

Roy Ebsary was charged with second degree murder concerning the killing of Sandy Seale, on May 12, 1983. After a short series of trials, he was convicted of manslaughter on January 17, 1985. He was sentenced to three years in prison. After an appeal was launched, the Nova Scotia Supreme Court upheld the conviction, but reduced the sentence to one year, which he eventually served.

The Royal Commission on the Donald Marshall Jr. Prosecution

The commissioners were not impressed by the police work done the night of the murder. In part, they criticized the four officers in the two cars that arrived on the scene:

> They did not cordon off the crime scene, search the area or question witnesses. In fact, none of the four officers dispatched to the scene even remained to protect the area after Seale had been taken to the hospital. We found their conduct entirely inadequate, incompetent and unprofessional (1989, p. 2)

They had the same harsh words for MacIntyre's performance as well (1989, p. 20). In addition, they concluded that he:

> without any evidence to support his conclusions and in the face of evidence to the contrary, had identified Marshall as the prime suspect by the morning of May 29, 1971...[and] accepted evidence that supported his conclusion and rejected evidence that discounted that

conclusion...[He] should not have ignored the statements given by George and Sandy MacNeil, which
described two men fitting the descriptions given by
Marshall in the part at the time of the incident...[And
he] failed to pursue efforts to locate the two men Marshall had described as being involved in Seale's
killing. (1989, p. 20)

They were also quite critical concerning the proceedings at the appeal hearing that eventually freed Marshall, especially as the strategy they took would affect any
compensation that Marshall might receive:

The Court of Appeal's gratuitous comments about
Marshall's responsibility for his own conviction, and
its own conclusion that any miscarriage of justice was
more apparent than real played a critically important
role in Marshall's negotiations with the Department
of Attorney George for compensation for his wrongful conviction. (1989, p. 7)

Recommendations

In a section entitled "Nova Scotia Micmac and the
Criminal Justice System," part of the larger part of the report
called "Recommendations," the Royal Commission on the
Donald Marshall Jr. Prosecution made the following recommendations. The commissioners recommended the establishment of a "community controlled Native Criminal Court" in
Nova Scotia as a five-year pilot project. This would entail having in at least a few reserves Native justices of the peace to
hear cases and applying culturally appropriate diversion and
meditation. They also recommended the establishment of a
Native Justice Institute, funded by both the federal and the
provincial governments. This would entail the training of
Mi'kmaq interpreters, and Mi'kmaq court workers, among
other educational endeavours. Also important to the commissioners was that there be regular sittings of the Provincial
Court in reserves, with the judges involved seeking the advice
of Native Justice Committees concerning sentencing of Aboriginal people that are convicted. The composition of juries
was also considered. They encouraged the initiation of a study

looking the need for proportional representation of Aboriginal people and other visible minorities on juries. Recall that in Marshall's case, all of the jurors were white.

In the Marshall case, the lawyers defending him were subjects of criticism by the commissioners. They felt that Nova Scotia Legal Aid be funded with monies directed to culturally sensitizing lawyers and to hiring Aboriginal social workers to act as liaisons between lawyers and their Mi'kmaq clients.

Finally, with respect to the policing of reserves, the commissioners recommended that both the RCMP and municipal police forces (such as the Cape Breton Regional Police Service) begin to actively recruit and hire Aboriginal Constables.

Policing Membertou Since the Donald Marshall Inquiry

The policing of the Membertou First Nation developed through three different stages since the Donald Marshall Inquiry: Unama'ki Tribal Police Force; RCMP; and Cape Breton Regional Police Service.

On July 12, 1994, the Unama'ki (based on the Mi'kmaq word for Cape Breton) Police Force came into operational existence. It was the first stand-alone First Nations police service in Atlantic Canada. In 1995, nine First Nations recruits graduated from the RCMP academy in Regina. After taking recruit training under RCMP supervision in Nova Scotia, they became the central core of the Unama'ki Tribal Police Force (UTPF).

The UTPF served not only Membertou First Nation, but four other Mi'kmaq communities as well: Chapel Island, Eskasoni, Wagmatcook, and Waycobah. Eskasoni, as the largest community (a population around 3,000 at the time) had the largest number and greatest variety of personnel: chief of police, sergeant, corporal, school liaison constable, court liaison constable, the constables, chief dispatcher and four other dispatchers, a secretary, and, for the local jail, two matrons, five jail guards, and a supervisor of the guards. Chapel Island had a corporal and a constable. The Membertou substation had a corporal and two constables. Waycobah had a corporal and a constable who served as the public relations officer.

The UTPF did not last long–only seven years. In March 2001, it was announced that the force was being phased out, and by the following April it was disbanded. Financial constraints were cited as the main reasons, but it seems that officer turnover related to living and working conditions, the rigours of servicing a large area, and the increasing demands of the serviced communities also were factors (Clairmont & McMillan, 2006).

A survey of Aboriginal police officers by C.J. Murphy and D. Clairmont published in 1996 revealed that there was a great deal of pressure put on people policing their own community (as was the case with 47% of the officers surveyed). The most common problem that was cited by these officers related to the strong social connections that existed in the community:

> [T]hey will expect you to "take their side," and "people take things personally." The officer has to deal with stresses and pressures related to bias and favouritism and with associated community expectations and perceptions; even if there is no bias, actions may be subject to that definition. (Murphy & Clairmont, 1996)

Fear of reprisals was a significant concern for Aboriginal officers working in stand-alone (as opposed to RCMP or other service affiliated). According to Murphy and Clairmont,

> [T]he reprisal reportedly could be directed at the officers' family members or material property or could be a loss of friendship; small-minded local politicians [e.g., chiefs and council members] could be especially vengeful. (Murphy & Clairmont, 1996)

It was noted in a study in 2001 by the First Nations Chiefs of Police Association that the small size of stand-alone Aboriginal police services was a subject of concern regarding promotions and other job benefits:

> The very small First Nations Self-Administered Po-
> lice Service lacks the positive offerings of a larger
> service and consequently has to manage a constant
> turnover in all the positions with the Police Service.
> (First Nations Chiefs of Police Association, 2001, 5.4,
> "Recruitment and Hiring")

In April 2002, the RCMP took over. They were in
charge of policing the Membertou First Nation until 2007
when the community signed an agreement with the Cape Breton Regional Police Service (CBRPS). At the time, it was
stated that reasons for the switch involved a cheaper price
(roughly $800,000 a year), a larger complement of officers
(seven rather than the five provided by the RCMP) in the
Membertou division, and a commitment to the CBRPS taking
courses on Mi'kmaq culture.

There could also be a sense, although we do not know
whether this is the case, that there was discrimination against
Aboriginal officers. The reason that this is mentioned here is
what was reported in Murphy and Clairmont's study in 1996,
when 128 Aboriginal RCMP officers were surveyed concerning what they believed were the weaknesses of their position
as Aboriginal officers in the RCMP:

> By far the most frequent shortfall was considered to
> be discrimination and racism from non-aboriginal fel-
> low officers and reflected in the policies and practices
> of the organization. It was widely contended that "na-
> tive police officers are not recognized or treated
> equally." Officers frequently claimed that supervisors
> and middle management officers exhibited racism in
> their promotion practices and in the assignment of re-
> sponsibilities. One member observed "white superi-
> ors use policy to go against native members yet they
> break policy and get away with it" while another
> claimed "the RCMP has a two tiered system, one for
> regular members in non-aboriginal positions while
> condescending to those in aboriginal positions."
> (Murphy & Clairmont, 1996)

No concrete commitment was made at the time to hiring First Nations officers. At the signing of the five-year

agreement, Chief Terence (Terry) Paul (the godson of Donald Marshall Sr.) stated.

> It's a very important day for Membertou…It's a new police service, but it's a service that has been with us ever since we've been a community. There have been a lot of positive things with the Cape Breton Regional Police and we like how they do things and we've been able to develop a good relationship with them.

The other communities that were part of the UTPF were at the time served by local detachments of the RCMP. In January, 2010, the band council of the Wagmatcook First Nation also switched over the CBRPS. The relationship between the community and the RCMP had been strained since one of their officers had shot a resident of the community. An inquest determined that the shooting was in self-defence.

As of 2012, the Mi'kmaq community of Listuguj Mi'gmaq Government (formerly known as Restigouche) in the Gaspé region of Quebec, with a population of roughly 3,400 (about 2,000 of those in community), have a police department as part of the Listuguj Public Security Directorate. (They have fire services and wildlife directorates as well.) They are one of three Mi'kmaq bands in Quebec, all in the Gaspé region. In 1981, the Sûreté du Quebec (SQ) raided the community concerning its fishing rights (see Abenaki filmmaker Alanis Obomsawin's 1984 documentary *Incident at Restigouche*), causing serious hard feelings between the SQ (who are the provincial police in Quebec) and the Mi'kmaq of this community.

The Mi'kmaq Justice Institute

In part as a response to the recommendation of the Marshall Inquiry that the federal and provincial governments fund a Native justice institute, the Mi'kmaq Justice Institute was formed in January 1997. Significantly, it was based in the Membertou/Sydney area. It developed three principal justice programs: Native Court Worker Program (NCWP), the Mi'kmaq Young Offender Project (MYOP), and the Etui-Nsitmek Translation Service (ENTS).

Unfortunately, although it began with great fanfare, it lasted only until the spring of 1999. Its problems, as addressed in Clairmont and McMillan's analysis in 2001, were several. Although core administrative funding was part of the problem, the heart of the problem was, in the analysts' eyes, that

> it quickly, and in hindsight prematurely and inadvisably, became involved in a large number of projects and activities. Program supervision suffered and serious organizational problems were allowed to fester, at least partly because the MJI leadership tried to accomplish too much too quickly. (Clairmont & McMillan, 2001, p. iv)

Interestingly, as well, when Mi'kmaq community members were interviewed, they seemed to be saying, more than they had in an earlier study done in 1992, that the mainstream justice system was appearing to be more responsive to the concerns of Mi'kmaq people (although they still believed that prejudice and stereotyping still existed in the system) (Clairmont & McMillan, 2001, p. viii). Further, they were also becoming "more sceptical concerning the potential advantages of a parallel Mi'kmaq justice system" (Clairmont & McMillan, 2001, p. ix).

In terms of the future, the program that seems to have been considered the most valuable and most necessary for the future was Mi'kmaq Young Offender Project. This relates to the predictability of the crime rates in the communities staying high, particularly concerning "property crime committed by youth." It relates as well to the way in which justice or sentencing circles were being considered appropriate diversions for such crimes, as opposed to violent crimes, which the Mi'kmaq people interviewed tended to see as best handled by the mainstream system.

Not a Panacea

The concept of a **panacea** (pronounced pan-ah-see-a) is that of a simple cure-all, a ready, perfect answer for any question or problem. The weakness of the concept of panacea generally is that the situations that bring about the challenges are not that simple. The cures for the ills need to be more complex and diversified, responding to each situation in unique ways. Aboriginal-run has been conceived of by many, Aboriginal and non-Aboriginal, as a kind of panacea. Many have thought that in dealing with a justice system that is systemically racist, all you have to do is have Aboriginal people run the police, the courts, and so on, in a parallel system, and the problems will soon disappear. Thinking such as that is not realistic or practical. Aboriginal-run comes with its own set of problems; plus, it needs to establish a good working relationship in various places with the larger, more powerful mainstream justice system. Aboriginal-run police services, for example, have to work with the RCMP, the various provincial policing services, and with city and town police. They need to cope with the sometimes petty politics of the band and especially with locally powerful politicians who can dominate a reserve, with negative effects on the Aboriginal policing service (who ultimately may be working for them). On the other side of the coin, the mainstream system can have players who are willing to let Aboriginal-run organizations "twist in the wind" to show that they are no better than the mainstream systems, that the old-style **paternalism** was right.

As Aboriginal-run systems are created and tested, much will be and has been learned and improved, much needs to be changed. **Best practices** of Aboriginal-run are being established and applied in a variety of situations. But there are also "worst practices," to be avoided once their weaknesses are discovered. You need to have Aboriginal-run "plus." What I mean by that is plus creativity, plus practicality, plus experience, plus a good working relationship with the mainstream system, plus a willingness to admit to and "own" failure.

Best Practices: Kitigan Zibi Anishinabeg First Nation Policing[2]

Best practices teach us about what can work in a given situation. A good example of such a practice concerning Aboriginal policing comes from the Kitigan Zibi Police Department (KZPD). Kitigan Zibi (translated as "Garden River") Anishinabeg First Nation is Algonquin, the largest of the nine Algonquin communities in Quebec and Ontario, with a band population of 2,886 as of March 2012. It is located in Quebec, about 130 kilometres north of Ottawa.

Three years after the Amerindian Police Service was developed in 1978, a program unique to Quebec, the Kitigan Zibi Anishinabeg First Nation took advantage of acquiring the limited authority that it gave to individual bands, through the creation of what were termed "Special Constables," not the equals of "real" constables in non-Aboriginal communities. In the words of an Aboriginal study of Aboriginal policing, "Despair was felt in the early days of Amerindian policing when officers were identified as 'Special Constables'" (First Nations Chiefs of, 2001). By 1985, the community stepped up to greater independence and authority by transferring their policing to their own force. Following the introduction of the federal First Nation Policing Policy, in April 1992, the community entered into a three-year tripartite (three parties—federal, provincial, and Aboriginal) policing agreement. This allowed the KZPD to become a fully functional force, the equivalent of a "normal" Canadian police service for a town or small city. The agreement has been extended into the present.

Their success is demonstrated in several ways. They early received in surveys a relatively high satisfaction rate from their community, something that is not a given in an Aboriginal police service. Second, the First Nations Chiefs of Police Association (FNCPA) survey of First Nations Self-Administered Police Services such as the KZPD, web-published in 2001, chose the KZPD as one of two such services chosen for best practices examples.

What factors have let to their success? Some of the factors could not be applied to many other communities. One is that, the community has long had a stable political environment, with little of the factionalism of families in and out of power that too frequently occurs in Aboriginal band/reserve politics. This would diminish the chances of clashes between chief and council and police force. Second, the KZPD has had a long, relatively positive relationship with the Sûreté du Québec (SQ), the Quebec provincial police, something not many Aboriginal police forces have in that province.

The KZPD have used several strategies that can be applied by other Aboriginal police services. One is their policy of developing a positive relationship with the youth of the community. In 1995, the KZAPD was one of four forces, the

only Aboriginal force to be engaged in a pilot project mentoring Aboriginal youth aged 12 to 24. Youth were paired with a
police officer, riding in cruisers, observing police duties and
practices first-hand, visiting the officer's home, and travelling
with the officer in various outings (e.g., sporting events). One
officer was quoted as saying, "I took great pride in seeing the
barriers fall and the sense of openness that developed in our
communication" (*First Nations Policing Update*, 1995). In a
1996 interview with the long-term police chief of the KZAPD
(still police chief in 2013), Gordon MacGregor, he stressed
"the importance of being among the people, being visible and
approachable especially to the youth and young children…
People see you as being human and as a father, not just as a
police figure" (MacGregor as cited in Stewart, 1996).

　　A third factor involved making sure that the training
and retraining of police officers of the KZAPD was equal to
that of officers in non-Aboriginal forces, enabling them to
conduct investigations throughout the province. They are
taught at the Ecolé National de Police du Québec, along with
officers from the other police services in the province.

Qualifying Statements

　　No police service is perfect, and that is, of course,
true for the KZPD. There are two issues now that challenge
them, issues they face along with non-Aboriginal police
forces. One is the issue of missing Aboriginal women. There
are two young women, Shannon Alexander and Maisy Odjick,
both 17 when they disappeared in 2008. There have been accusations that the KZPD has not been as active in pursuing
these disappearances as perhaps they should, that they are
compromised by their connection to the SQ in this regard.
This latter point seems more apparently the case with a more
contentious issue. In 2001, a 61-year-old Algonquin woman,
Gladys Tolley, was killed when she was struck by an SQ police vehicle patrolling the Kitigan Zibi Anishinabeg First Nation reserve. Her daughter Bridget Tolley has suggested that
the SQ was acting beyond its jurisdiction in patrolling the territory of the KZPD, that the SQ was acting with a conflict of
interests in its investigation, and that the KZPD has insufficiently challenged the SQ in the matter.

Mi'kmaq Legal Support Network

The Mi'kmaq Legal Support Network (MLSN) is a justice support system whose clients are Aboriginal people involved in the Nova Scotia justice system. As the only Aboriginal bands in Nova Scotia are Mi'kmaq, they are almost exclusively their only clientele. Its main programs are the Mi'kmaq Court Worker and Mi'kmaq Customary Law Programs. On its website, it declares the following to be its core purpose:

> Since its inception, MLSN has always attempted to make a non-Mi'kmaq system of justice better for Aboriginal people in Nova Scotia. This system is largely process oriented and lacking Aboriginal cultural values. MLSN programs and services help bridge these gaps but [it] is often found that the criminal justice system needs to be more receptive to Mi'kmaq concepts of justice (www.eskasoni.ca/Departments/12/)

The MLSN is based in Eskasoni, a community whose name is based on the Mi'kmaq word We'kwistoqnik, meaning "where the fir trees are plentiful." It is the largest Mi'kmaq community not only in Nova Scotia but in all of Canada, as during the 1940s, the federal government exercised a program of centralization, taking Mi'kmaq families from other areas and forcibly moving them to Eskasoni. As of March 2012, it had a registered band population of 4,087, about 3,500 of whom live in community.

The Mi'kmaq Bounty: Still Unresolved

When, in 1749, British Colonel Edward Cornwallis led more than 2,400 English-speaking intruders to settle on the east coast of Nova Scotia, where Halifax is today, but which was the heart of Mi'kmaq country at the time, the Mi'kmaq responded with armed resistance. Cornwallis in return declared war on the people and put a bounty on their heads, initially £10, later £50, a significant sum. They were wanted dead or alive; a scalp would suffice as evidence for payment. There is a general principle in Canadian law that works like this. Any law that was passed by the British government or one of its colonial agents (such as Cornwallis), unless it was specifically contravened, remained law in the Canada of 1867 and later. Using this principle, it would appear that, at least technically, the bounty on the Mi'kmaq still holds.

The Nova Scotia government sent a "Resolution on Bounty Proclamation" on March 28, 2000 to the federal government, asking it to take action to remove the bounty from the books. The Mi'kmaq had requested that as part of a new round of treaty negotiations at the time. Over the years, I have tried to find whether that the bounty was actually removed. I have been phone bounced back and forth between people working for the Nova Scotia and federal governments and eventually learned that an announcement was written up at some point, but we could not find any actual concrete evidence that the bounty had been removed.

Wilson Nepoose

Wilson Nepoose has been referred to as Alberta's Donald Marshall. The Cree man from the Samson Band was in his early forties when he was arrested in July 1986, a few years after Marshall was released. The crime he was charged with was the strangulation of Rose Marie Desjarlais of Edmonton. The physical evidence against him was weak. He was convicted in 1987 on the strength of the testimonies of two women. One of those women has since died, but the other one has been sentenced for two years concerning her false testimony in this case. She claimed that she was pressured by the RCMP into lying to help them make their conviction.

In 1990, Jack Ramsay would take up the case for the Nepoose family as an investigator. It was unusual that he did so as he was earlier involved with the case as an RCMP officer, and he was then a Reform Party Member of Parliament, not a party known for having sympathy concerning Aboriginal issues. Ramsay said the following:

> I was involved with the case before I was elected and
> I know from the evidence…I'm one of the few people
> who has looked at the evidence from front to end and
> I know that Wilson Nepoose was not guilty of the

> murder he was convicted of and I know that he spent five years in jail for a crime he didn't commit. (as cited in Barnsley, 1999, p. 1)

The evidence he put together was so compelling that the very conservative and usually anti-Native weekly, the *Alberta Report*, wrote a cover story entitled "White Man's Justice: New Evidence" that questioned the conviction.

In 1992, the conviction was overturned in the Alberta Court of Appeals. The judge said that Nepoose's conviction had been his conviction was a "miscarriage of justice." In 1993, a petition was presented to Ralph Klein, the Alberta premier, with 7,500 signatures (in the days before on-line petitions) to have an inquiry. It never happened.

In 1997, Nepoose was reported missing, and his skeletal remains were discovered in January 1998—death by apparent suicide.

Donald Marshall Jr. Faces the Law Again and Wins

Junior would have another major standoff with the law. In August 1993, he was arrested for three violations of the provincial Fisheries Act. He was charged with fishing without a license, fishing out of season with nets deemed illegal, and of selling eels without a license. He did not deny what he had done because it was an act of protest, trying to draw attention to Mi'kmaq treaty rights. He told the court that he had caught 463 pounds of eels during the closed season and then sold them for slightly less than $800. He asserted, however, that he was not breaking the law, as he claimed rights under a treaty signed in 1760 between the British Crown and the Mi'kmaq and two related peoples, the Malecite and the Passamaquoddy.

The case would go through increasingly higher levels of courts. He was convicted on all three charges, and these convictions were later upheld in the Nova Scotia Court of Appeal. The convictions were then overturned by the Supreme Court of Canada on September 17, 1999, as the judges there recognized that the treaty granted the people the right to fish and to trade products from hunting, fishing, and trapping. For them, the key word in the treaty was "necessaries," meaning in their interpretation that a Mi'kmaq family had the federally-given right to produce a "moderate livelihood'" from fishing, regardless of provincial fishing laws.

This victory brought forward a fight for lobster fishing between non-Aboriginal license holders and the Mi'kmaq, that at times grew violent and put the Mi'kmaq in the news for a period of about two years. An agreement with the federal government was arranged.

The End

Marshall's last few years were not pleasant ones. In 2003, Donald Marshall Jr. received a double lung transplant. Failing to take the appropriate medicine, or mixing that medicine with alcohol, and, most probably, the effects of 11 years in prison, led to Junior have conflict with the law over violence with other Mi'kmaq. He had to leave his home community to live out the rest of his life in Eskasoni. On August 6, 2009, he died from complications related to that transplant.

Conclusions

We have seen in the Donald Marshall Jr. case that the personal racism of the leading investigating officer, plus the institutional of systemic racism of the justice system in Nova Scotia, contributed to a miscarriage of justice in which an innocent man, a Mi'kmaq teenager, was imprisoned for 11 years for a crime that he did not commit. Even with his acquittal in the first inquiry there were attempts to blame the victim rather than the system for the injustice that took place.

We have also seen that three different policing services have been employed in succession to provide a system for Marshall's home community, Membertou First Nation, that is fair, just, and efficient. The first system employed was the Unama'ki Tribal Police Force (UTPF), a stand-alone tribal police force, that, unfortunately, only last for seven years (1994 to 2001). This demonstrated that, among other things, just shifting to tribal police is not a panacea that will work in every instance unless some complications are addressed. Secondly, the RCMP took over from 2001 to 2007, but were replaced by Cape Breton Regional Police Service in 2007.

The injustice on the scale of the Donald Marshall Jr. case is highly unlikely to repeat itself in the future, as some significant changes have been made (including Mi'kmaq cultural training for police officers, Mi'kmaq court workers, and legal organizations). Further, his successful appeal led to changes in the Evidence Act in Canada, ending Crown prosecutors' capacity to, at their discretion, present or not present to the defence attorneys evidence that they had uncovered. Still, it remains to be seen whether this is enough to make up a fair system of justice for the Mi'kmaq people of Membertou First Nation.

Questions

1. Do you think that the Nova Scotia statistics reflect more systemic or personal racism?
2. Do you think that if we had execution still in Canada, the racial figures would be just about the same as they were when there was execution?
3. What do you think that the Cape Breton Region Police Service needs to do to avoid the apparent failures of the previous policing systems in Membertou?
4. There are a good number of websites that argue that Marshall should be blamed for initiating the series of actions that led to the murder. Why do you think that this is?
5. Donald Marshall Jr. received $250,000 compensation for the miscarriage of justice that affected him. Do you think that this is reasonable or is it too much or too little?
6. Do you foresee any problems with the return of the Cape Breton Regional Police Service to policing Membertou First Nation?
7. Do you think that the Restigouche police service has a better chance of survival than did the Unama'ki Tribal Police Force (UTPF)? Explain.
8. How do you think the problems mentioned concerning the Unama'ki Tribal Police Force and other small Aboriginal stand-alone or self-administered police services can be dealt with?
9. During the time of the UTPF, it was ruled in court in the case of a non-Aboriginal speeder that their constables had authority off reserve. This is similar to rulings in British

Columbia, to name one jurisdiction. What do you think was the non-Aboriginal response to that?

10. How might the story of the failure of the Mi'kmaq Justice Institute be helpful concerning the success or failure of independent Mi'kmaq policing services?

11. If a new organization were to development that was similar to Mi'kmaq Justice Institute, how should it be different from the original organization?

12. Treaty and Aboriginal rights are federal, while game and fishing laws are within the jurisdiction of the provinces. How would you recommend these two sides be balanced in terms of such issues as fishing and hunting seasons, and selling of fish and game for money?

13. Why has a clear proclamation not been made about the Mi'kmaw bounty? What do you think that the role of not wanting to draw attention to the racist background of some of our laws has to do with this issue?

Key Terms

best practices–strategies with a proven history of achieving desired results more effectively or consistently than similar methods used in the past by a particular organization or currently by other organizations in the same industry.

panacea–an uncomplicated basic solution that is unrealistically believed to automatically resolve a broad set of problems.

paternalism–a way of treating people as if they were childhood, incapable of handling the basic responsibilities over their lives.

racializing clemency–a process in which the convicted who belong to a negatively valued racialized group tend to receive stiffer sentences than other convicted people.

racial devaluing (of the killer and the victim)–processes in which members of the negatively valued racialized group receive stiffer sentences as convicted killers, and in which membership in such a group as a victim lessens the sentence delivered.

Notes

[1]   They currently have four reserves, two small ones essentially in Sydney, two other larger ones farther away, one of which is shared with other Mi'kmaq bands. Recently (2012), land has been purchased upon which to build a new school.

[2]   Adapted from Cummins and Steckley (2003, pp. 123-125).

References

Avio, K.L. (1987). The quality of mercy: Exercise of the royal prerogative in Canada. *Canadian Public Policy, 12*, 366-379.

Barnsley, P. (1999). AFN pushes for inquiry into RCMP. *Windspeaker, 17*(7), 1.

Clairmont, D., & McMillan, J. (2001). *Directions in Mi'kmaq justice: An evaluation of the Mi'kmaq justice system and its aftermath.* Retrieved from http://www.gov.ns.ca/just/publications/docs/TFexesum.pdf

Clairmont, D., & McMillan, J. (2006). *Directions in Mi'kmaq justice: Notes on the assessment of the Mi'kmaq legal support network.* Presented to the Mi'kmaq Legal Support Network and the Tripartite Forum: Justice Subcommittee, Atlantic Institute of Criminology, Dalhousie University. Retrieved from http://sociologyandsocialanthropology.dal.ca

Comeau, P., & Santin, A. (1990). *The First Canadians–A profile of Canada's Native people today.* Toronto, ON: James Lorimer and Company.

Cummins, B.D., & Steckley, J.L. (2003). *Aboriginal policing: A Canadian perspective.* Toronto: Prentice-Hall.

Eskasoni First Nation. About us. Retrieved from http://www.eskasoni.ca/About/

Eskasoni First Nation. The Mi'kmaq legal support network. Retrieved from http://www.eskasoni.ca/Departments/12

First Nations Chiefs of Police Association and Human Resources Development Canada. (2001). *A human resource study of First Nations policing in Canada.* Retrieved from http://www.soonet.ca/fncpa/hrdc

First Nations Policing Update. (1995, July, no. 3.) Aboriginal Policing Directorate, Solicitor General Canada. Catalogue no. JS42-58/3-1995.

Harris, M. (1986). *Justice denied: The law versus Donald Marshall.* Toronto, ON: Macmillan.

Hayes, C. (2007). Membertou to be patrolled. *Cape Breton Post,* June 23.

Hickman, T.A., Poitras, L.A., & Evans, G.T. (1989). *Royal commission on the Donald Marshall, Jr., prosecution.* Province of Nova Scotia.

Murphy, C.J., & Clairmont, D. (1996). *First Nations Police Officers survey.* Solicitor General Canada. Retrieved from http://www.sgc.gc.ca/epub/Abo/e199606/e199606.htm

Obomsawin, A. (1984). *Incident at Restigouche.* Documentary film. National Film Board.

Stewart, S. (1996). A day in the life of two community police officers: The Aboriginal Police directorate takes a look at the First Nations policing policy in action.

York, G. (1990). *The dispossessed: Life and death in Native Canada.* London, ON: Vintage.

Chapter 4

The Minnie Sutherland Case

There is an equation of being drunk, Indian and in prison. Like many stereotypes, this one has a dark underside. It reflects a view of native people as uncivilized and without a coherent social or moral order. The stereotype prevents us from seeing native people as equals. (Michael Jackson, 1989, as cited in Rudin, 2007)

Cree playwright Tomson Highway wrote concerning the drunk "Indian" on the streets of a town or city:

That is the first and only way most white people see Indians...That's our national image. In fact, the average white Canadian has seen that visual more frequently than they've seen a beaver. To my mind, you might as well put an Indian drunk on the Canadian nickel. (as quoted in York, 1990, p. 191)

Mohawk author Brian Maracle, in his book *Crazywater*, wrote:

When I think about the National Native Alcohol and Drug Abuse Program, I can't help thinking that we, as native people, have the dubious distinction of being the only race of people in the country to have a government program geared to combat our alcoholism. Think of it! There are no special programs to deal with other ethnic groups in spite of their legendary fondness for beer, wine, vodka, scotch or whiskey.

The very existence of the program is a slap in the face. It diminishes our self-esteem by contributing to the misperception that "all native people are drunks." (Maracle, 1994, p. 11)

Richard W. Thatcher, in his book *Fighting Firewater Fictions: Moving beyond the Disease Model of Alcoholism in First Nations* (2004), writes,

"the phrase 'drunken Indian' reflects one of the most common and enduring ethnic stereotypes not only in Canada but in North America as a whole." (p. 15)

Marjorie Hodgson is a Nadleh Whuten Carrier elder from northern British Columbia. She is a leading figure in the development of Aboriginal programs to fight alcohol and substance abuse. When she was a teenager, she was raped by a white businessman. The RCMP officer investigating the crime downplayed the importance of this traumatic event by saying to Hodgson's mother,

"You're an alcoholic and an Indian…and so is she. She's there to be used." (as cited in Wadden, 2008, p. 13)

Standing in the Shadow of an Awfully Big Stereotype

The Minnie Sutherland story is about alcohol and "Indians." But it was not alcohol that killed Minnie Sutherland; it was the nature of the cultural stereotype that links Aboriginal people and alcohol that was the leading factor in her death. To the police, she was "just another drunken Indian." It was part of the mistaken idea that Aboriginal people do not drink with any moderation or control; they just get drunk. The false notion dictates that they have no choice. It is part of the unfortunate idea that when many people look at an Aboriginal person that is drinking or drunk, they think, "There is a drunk Indian," while when they look at a white person who is drunk, they think, "There is a drunk." When it comes to being an Aboriginal person, you can be denied being seen as an individual or as a complex individual with a variety of social statuses because you are standing in the shadow of an awfully big stereotype. It casts darkness over other, more positive, aspects of what you are.

Aboriginal peoples did not have alcohol before Europeans came to this country with their cheap liquid trade goods, initially wine (from the French) and rum (from the English). Some of the Aboriginal terms for alcohol reflect its foreign nature. A Carrier (a Dene language) term for alcohol is *nedo*, which roughly translated means "white man's water" (Maracle, 1994, p. 24).

The manufacture of alcohol typically develops in cultures involved with farming crops on a fairly large scale, and the vast majority of cultures in pre-contact Aboriginal Canada were hunters and gatherers, sometimes known to anthropologists as foragers. Those Aboriginal groups in southern Ontario and southern Quebec who farmed grew corn, beans, and squash used these products only for food. It does not seem that there were any "recreational drugs" either, nothing stronger than the powerful tobacco that could make the inexperienced feel dizzy.

The stereotype of the Indian drunk has been socially constructed over several centuries. How alcohol was introduced to the Aboriginal people, how Aboriginal interaction with alcohol was early reported in writings by the French and English, how the laws with respect to Aboriginal people and alcohol were vastly different from the laws that related to other Canadians in that regard are all players in the construction of the stereotype.

The fur trade gave the stereotype its foundation. The fur trade is one of the few Canadian historical images or institutions that many Canadians actually know something about. It is part of the ideology of how "we built this land," the first step followed by the broad strides of the construction of the country-wide railroad. When the image of the fur trade incorporates and shows some measure of respect for Aboriginal people, it is an image of two people working together, which, to be fair, it sometimes was. Certainly, that was the case in the early days before alcohol found its way into the fur trade. However, the cold-hearted exploitation of Aboriginal trading "partners" through alcohol factor needs to be considered as well. Alcohol had a better profit margin for European traders than other materials, about which Aboriginal traders could be and often were hard bargainers. And people would only trade for just so many axes, guns, and Hudson's Bay blankets. Alcohol is quickly consumed and needs to be purchased again and again, unlike many other trade good supplies.

And when, during the eighteenth and early nineteenth centuries, there was competition between the English-run Hudson's Bay Company (HBC) and the Montreal-centred Northwest Company (NWC), the amount of alcohol poured into the trade was literally staggering. At York Factory, a major HBC trading post by the west coast of Hudson Bay, 864 gallons of rum was traded in 1753. During the period of 1720 to 1774, 21,634 gallons of that cheaply produced alcohol were traded from that post alone (Steckley & Cummins, 2001, p. 180). The figures only lowered somewhat when the two companies merged in 1822, but the basic pattern had been established.

It should be pointed out that Aboriginal people were long well-aware of the destructive force alcohol had on their families, friends, and communities, and many fought to oppose it. For example, the devastation alcohol had on the people is ably described by the Reverend Peter Jacobs or Pahtahsegua, a Mississauga (Anishinabe) preacher, teacher, and author from southern Ontario in 1836:

> [My] father and mother died when I was very young, in drinking the fire water1 to excess...My sister and brother-in-law then took me to bring me up. But in a short time they died also in drinking the fire water to excess. My sister was frozen to death on a drinking spree, on new year's day...And in about one year from this time one of my sisters, in a drunken spree, was struck with a club on her head by her husband, which caused her death. And in the same year my brother was tomahawked in a drinking spree. (Schmalz, 1991, p. 133)

Unfortunately, the difficulty of his battle to be able to walk tall in two worlds overwhelmed him. He, too, became another sad story, another "Indian" statistic documenting the ravages of alcohol on the people.

Historical Portrait: Heroic Mounties and Drunk Indians at Fort Whoop-Up

In his excellent and informative work, *The Imaginary Indian: The Images of the Indian in Canadian Culture* (1992), historian Daniel Francis discusses how the positive historical image of the Mounties has come at the cost of negative imaging of Aboriginal people. Francis contends that one story that contributes to this negative imaging is the depiction of the Mountie as the white saviour of the drunken Indian who is victimized by the unscrupulous American whisky traders at the place nicknamed "Fort Whoop-Up" (near present day Lethbridge) Alberta in 1874. While there is some truth to the story that the North West Mounted Police (NWMP, who would later become the RCMP), formed in 1873, did act bravely and effectively in taking on the often well-armed American traders, the image of the drunken and helpless Indian is an exaggeration of their more complex roles in that situation.

Paternalistic Laws and Alcohol among Aboriginal People

Paternalism refers to a way of dealing with people as if you (as an individual or government body) are a parent who knows best, and the people are kept in a kind of long-term childhood. Paternalism keeps people from socially maturing so that they can handle their own problems. For a long time, Canada's laws on Aboriginal people and alcohol clearly reflected a paternalistic position. The Indian Act was put into place initially in 1876. Parts of the Indian Act strictly restricted Native contact with alcohol. Section 94 of the Indian Act read as follows:

> 94. An Indian who
>   a) has intoxicants in his possession,
>   b) is intoxicated, or
>   c) makes or manufactures intoxicants off a reserve,
>
>   is guilty of an offence and is liable on summary conviction to a fine of not less than ten dollars and not more than fifty dollars or to imprisonment for term not exceeding three months to both fine and imprisonment.

One of the 75 Aboriginal people that Brian Maracle interviewed for his book, *Crazywater*, was a 31-year-old Cree woman. She told Maracle (a Mohawk) of what the situation was like (before drinking was legal) to have the police come to your door when you were suspected of drinking. Her parents were drinking homebrew (a common strategy when you could not buy alcohol). There was a loud knock from the police at the door. Her parents turned off the light (a coal oil lamp) so that it was

> pitch dark in the house and I got scared and the police, they knocked the door down. They literally kicked it down on the floor and they searched the whole place. They had these big flashlights. They searched the whole place looking for booze, and my parents, they stashed it, and the police they didn't find the booze.
>
> I was just a kid but it's just like it happened yesterday. I remember 'cause I was terrified. (Maracle, 1994, p. 50)

If you were a "status Indian" and you wanted to drink, the only legal way in which you could do so was to become enfranchised, that meant you lost your status as a officially "Indian," lose your treaty and basic Aboriginal rights, including at least potentially being kicked out of your reserve home. You were separated from your people. In *Crazywater*, Maracle tells the story of how his father became enfranchised because of his desire for alcohol, a move that brought a wave of alcohol problems to his family (Maracle, 1994, pp. 3-4).

Section 94 of the Indian Act was successfully challenged in the *Regina v. Drybones* case. Joseph Drybones, a Dene, had been charged under Section 94(b) for being intoxicated in a hotel bar in Yellowknife, Northwest Territories, on April 8, 1967. As Section 94(b) differed significantly from the territorial Liquor Ordinance, Drybones's lawyers argued that this contravened the 1960 Canadian Bill of Rights. They won the case in 1969, liberalizing, at least technically (see below), alcohol-related laws concerning status Indians across the country.

This did not mean that people could necessarily legally drink on reserves. Until 1985, unless the chief and council voted specifically in favour of drinking being allowed in their community, it was not legal. After 1985, the situation was reversed, so that drinking was allowed unless the chief and council voted against it. There are technically "dry" reserves today. As recently as 2004, there were 22 dry reserves in Manitoba alone. There is an ongoing debate among Aboriginal leaders about whether making a reserve technically "alcohol-free" does more harm than good. Bootleggers bring in large amounts of alcohol with huge markup. In a 2011 case, in a technically "dry" reserve in northern Manitoba in which large amounts of alcohol were confiscated, an investigator hired by Indian Affairs found that a large bottle of whisky and two 24 cases of beer that cost about $115 in Winnipeg were bootlegged for $400 to $500 on the reserve. The chief of the reserve was implicated in using alcohol to bribe his way to a successful election (Turner, 2011).

And reserves that are dry can help contribute to the image and statistics of the drunken Indian. Anishinabe (Ojibwa) author Wilfred Pelletier writes about how that worked with towns and cities near reserves:

> There are still some reserves where drinking is against the law, so Indians go into town and buy a bottle or maybe two. They can't take it home and drink it, and it's against the law to drink in a public place. So what do they do? They go in a back alley or maybe in a men's can and they knock the whole bottle off real quick. So then there are some drunken Indians staggering around the town, because drinking that fast will knock anybody on his ass. (Pelletier & Poole, 1973, p. 90; see also Maracle, 1994, p. 47)

People also used to drink vanilla extract, aftershave, perfume, mouthwash, rubbing alcohol, Lysol–anything they could legally buy that had some amount of alcohol in it. And homebrew can be just as deadly (Canadian Press, 2009).

A good summary of this situation and what is needed for meaningful change comes from Anishinabe journalist Colleen Simard, who writes for the Winnipeg Free Press. In a 2010 article, entitled "Will a booze ban save the kids of Natuashish?" Simard writes about the Labrador community (known in English as Davis Inlet) that became momentarily famous in Canadian news in 1993 for television footage of its children sniffing gas out of garbage bags to get high. There had been a ban on alcohol since 2008 in Natuashish. Reported incidence of violence had dropped by about half, school attendance had gone up, and suicide rates had dropped, but alcohol related problems did not disappear, and seemed to have gone underground. Simard wrote:

> Attacking addiction by cutting off the legal supply of alcohol never works. In Natuashish you can buy a bottle of booze for about $350. I've been on many a dry reserve, and trust me: the drugs, alcohol and sniff still get in, ban or no ban. In fact, bans make people more creative–think of the homemade alcohol like "super juice," which is potentially more dangerous than regular booze.
>
> But an alcohol or drug ban can do some good if it is the community that is driving it and the ban is part of a plan to battle substance abuse... Only the community members themselves can fix their problem. (2010)

Over-Policing and Using Alcohol Laws to Target Aboriginal People

In his insightful report connected with the Ipperwash Inquiry,[2] *Aboriginal Peoples and the Criminal Justice System,* Jonathan Rudin refers to **over-policing** as "the practice by the police of focusing their attention inordinately in one particular geographic area (or neighbourhood) or on members on members of one particular racial or ethnic group" (Rudin, 2007, p. 28).

The key to over-policing lies in the **discretionary** powers that officers have, their ability to choose whether to charge someone with an offence, in the case we are talking about here, with alcohol related offences. According to Rudin, law officers have over-policed Aboriginal communities and individuals by applying the "drunk in public" laws that are in place in every major jurisdiction, provincial and territorial in Canada, but are usually not applied. A classic example he presents dates back to 1972.

The story takes place in Alert Bay, British Columbia, on the west side of Vancouver Island. The Nimpkish Reserve of the Kwawkewth (usually written in English, somewhat inaccurately, as Kwakiutl) people was a short distance away. When the people wanted to drink they would go to one particular bar where they felt they belonged. The local detachment of the RCMP would wait outside that bar and arrest those they determined to be "drunk in a public place," a policing practice that was not followed to a similar extent with bars where white people hung out. Arrested Kwawkewth would spend at least one night in jail, beginning or increasing their criminal record, and inflating the Aboriginal incarceration statistics. Over-policing leads to over-representation.

Enter law students from the University of British Columbia in Vancouver. They were working over the summer in the Nimpkish reserve. To prevent the arrests, and the consequent disruption of the community, the students had a bus running between the bar and the community at regular intervals, thus significantly lowering the number of arrests. The RCMP responded with the threat of charging the law students with obstructing justice. Fortunately, their law professor, Michael Jackson, who later wrote a key report on Aboriginal people and the law, intervened. He correctly informed the police that no laws were being broken by the use of the bus. His interpretation won out.

Sociologist David Stymeist details another instance of discriminatory discretion in the following quotation from his 16 months of experience studying "Ethnics and Indians" in "Crow Lake" (Kenora) in northwest Ontario in 1971 and 1972:

> Most arrests in Crow Lake are for public intoxication. Ontario Provincial Police cars park outside the entrance to the Crow Lake Hotel, the town's largest central pub, for an hour or so before and after the pub closes. The waiters will ask a drunk white man, who is perhaps a relative, friend or steady customer, if he wants to call a cab. The cab will arrive at the back door of the hotel and the man in question will leave unseen. Many Indians, however, are arrested as they leave the pub, and some have been arrested for public drunkenness as they were climbing the stairs to their rooms in the hotel. (Stymeist, 1975, p. 75)

A 1977 study conducted by the Saskatchewan Alcoholism Commission found that, of 3,368 people arrested for public drunkenness in the city of Regina, 62% were Aboriginal, despite the fact that they comprised only about 15% of the population of that city (Reid, Dewit, & Matonovich, 1980, as cited in Thatcher, 2004, p. 16). Of course, when people get arrested, and they seem to be cherry-picked for the arrest, they might be inclined to resist, which leads to further offences on their record. As Tim Quigley of the University of Saskatchewan put it in an article published in 1994,

> The police rarely arrest whites for being intoxicated in public. No wonder there is resentment on the part of Aboriginal people arrested simply for being intoxicated. This situation often results in an Aboriginal person being charged with obstruction, resisting arrest or assaulting a police officer. An almost inevitable consequence is incarceration. (Quigley, 1994, pp. 273-274)

The Story of Minnie Sutherland: Death by Stereotype?

This sad story begins on New Year's Eve, 1989, when Minnie Sutherland, a slight and short (just under five feet tall), mother of two (girls aged 19 and 9), 40-year-old Cree woman from Kashechewan in northern Ontario went out to meet a friend at about 11:00 p.m. to celebrate the New Year. They went first to one bar, and ended up in J. R. Dallas (named after a popular television show and its favourite villain), a country and western bar, where they had few drinks in what was known as the "Indian section" of the bar.

Some short hours after the turn of the new year, the 20 or so bars in the seedy two block area known to many in the capital area as a place to walk on the wild side, had just closed, at 3:00 a.m. (much later than on the Ottawa, Ontario side of the river), and had discharged their patrons into the street. Minnie and her cousin Joyce Wesley were standing on the sidewalk; Minnie was looking for a cab to take her back to Ottawa and her home. She had trouble seeing (she had been deemed legally blind) as she wore very thick glasses that did little more than enable her to sense what was around her.

It was about 3:30 a.m. Minnie, her cousin, and a few hundred others were milling around the street. As Minnie stepped into the street, looking for a cab, she fell, and then was struck by a car. Blue paint from the car rubbed off onto her coat. The car's driver and passenger were both off-duty nurses. They got out of their car when they heard the bump and saw Minnie fall. They checked her over, but were sure neither of her state, nor what had actually happened. Three male university students saw the accident and moved towards the scene to see if Minnie was okay.

Minnie's First Interaction with the Police

Two young male police officers noticed the sudden stoppage of traffic on the busy road and got out of their van to see what had happened. One of the students told them that a car had hit the woman. Then one of the officers asked Minnie's cousin what had happened to the woman he saw sprawled out in front of him. Minnie's cousin was not sure. The road and the sidewalks were crowded, and she had not actually seen the accident. Part of speaking truth in traditional Cree culture is to tell only that what you have directly experienced. She mentioned that she and her cousin had been drinking. For the officers, that single fact probably overrode thoughts of Minnie being a "victim" of an accident that required help. She became a "squaw," another drunken Indian. The officers then attempted to lift Minnie up to a sitting position. One of the university students was upset by this, knowing that accident victims should not be moved until medical help arrives, and shouted at the officers. One officer told the student to leave and said that he would be arrested if he did not keep quiet.

The officers asked the nurse who had been driving whether the car stopped was hers and requested that she move it. Keeping the traffic moving was important to them, seemingly more important than the Cree woman lying on the road. The nurses did not want to leave the scene of the accident until they knew for sure that Minnie was okay. Understandably, they wondered at the apparently casual attitude of the officer concerning an accident victim. According to author John Nihmey, who had access to the transcripts of the hearing that would follow Minnie Sutherland's death, the officers "were perplexed by what seemed to be an overreaction to a drunk woman who had either slipped on an ice patch and fallen, or walked into a car that couldn't have been going very fast given all the traffic" (Nihmey, 1998, pp. 82-83). According to the nurse whose car hit Minnie: They kept telling us to leave because there was a lot of traffic. They didn't care about her. They didn't even look at her (Nihmey, 1998, p. 73).

The officers picked Minnie up and deposited her at the side of the road. From eye-witness accounts, Nihmey described the procedure as follows:

> Shock registered on the faces of the people watching the officers move Minnie to the side of the road. Bystanders on the sidewalk saw the two officers lift Minnie from under the shoulders, pull her toward the side of the road, and set her down in the snow. Those closer to Minnie saw each officer grab a shoulder of her coat and drag her through the slush, arms dangling limp, heels bumping along the road, and head lolling back and forth, over to the side of the road. They dropped her in the snowbank. (Nihmey, 1998, p. 83)

One of the university students tried to call 911, but that service was not then available in Hull, so the attempt did not work. Then he asked Minnie's cousin, Joyce whether she wanted them to call a taxi. She said that she did. One of the students suggested an ambulance. That sounded to her like a better idea, so the cousin changed her mind and told the police that they should can an ambulance instead. The officer called into Hull Police Headquarters and said, "Cancel the taxi now. The squaw decided otherwise" (Nihmey, 1998, p. 84). The one word indicated their attitude: no respect. The police then left, feeling that they had completed their work there and had to return to other problems of that crowded area. The traffic must keep moving. The "squaw" was abandoned by the law.

The male university students and the two Cree women went into a restaurant. The students, perhaps feeling that Minnie was looking a little better (although she was barely conscious), and probably wanting to discharge their responsibility, then left. Two other men, seeing Indian women, squaws, as useful for one purpose, then picked up the two women and drove them to Ottawa. But coming to realize the sorry state that Minnie was in, they called 911 (which was available on the Ontario side of the Ottawa River) and dropped Minnie off beside a restaurant, taking her cousin with them. Minnie was alone, with no one to tell the story of her accident. She, herself, was unable because of the accident.

Minnie's Second Encounter with the Police

A female officer from the Ottawa police service responded to the successful 911 call. She tried to rouse Minnie to consciousness but failed. An ambulance pulled up and a paramedic, unaware of her earlier accident, checked Minnie over. After subjecting her to some basic medical tests, he stated that she was drunk (another drunk Indian?) and suggested that the officer take her to a detoxification centre. The paramedic then drove the ambulance away. Being Aboriginal and having consumed alcohol trumped any sense that anything else might be seriously wrong with the diminutive Cree woman.

The female officer dragged Minnie into the back of her car awkwardly and drove Minnie to the charity-run detox centre. The staff, however, would not admit her because of a policy of not taking in people who were unconscious or non-ambulatory (i.e., unable to walk). It was now about 5:00 a.m. The officer then drove Minnie to her station and conferred with her sergeant. He checked Minnie over, looking for possible signs of her being in a fight (that's what drunk Indians usually do) and recommended that the officer drive Minnie to a nearby hospital, the place of last resort in a number of Canadian cities for "drunk Indians."

Minnie arrived at the hospital at 5:45 a.m. The people at the hospital seemed to have just seen a drunk Aboriginal woman, not someone who had had an accident. Unfortunately, no one was there who could tell them otherwise.

On January 3, Patrick Smith, one of the university students, contacted both the hospital and the Hull police concerning the fact that Minnie had been in an accident. After going through a long chain of command at the police station, he finally was able to talk to Captain Armand Caron. When

Caron went to Smith's home shortly afterwards, he and a fellow officer merely questioned Smith about his "arrogant attitude" concerning the officers' moving an injured person. They also queried him about how much alcohol he and his companions had drunk prior to that time. Their intent was apparently restricted to defending the officers involved, not pursuit of the truth concerning the negligent police treatment of Minnie Sutherland.

Minnie stayed at the hospital until she died on January 11 of a cardiac arrest, the result of a blood clot in the back of her brain caused by her accident. The doctors at the hospital had been unaware of the blood clot and had not felt her case was serious enough to warrant an MRI (Magnetic Resonance Imaging). This was new technology at that hospital with a long waiting list. On January 17, Dr. Gwynne Jones, a doctor from the hospital sent the following letter to the Hull police:

> There is no doubt that the lack of information about the traumatic event was of great significance in making the initial diagnosis of the abnormality and in following this up to a logical conclusion which may have been able to prevent her demise.
>
> It is also unfortunate that Mrs. Sutherland received powerful antibiotics for her condition which would not have been necessary had this history been available. The antibiotics do have their own particular risks.
>
> In particular, if the allegations of the conduct of the Hull Police are correct, then a serious error of judgment has been made by the officers concerned and this should be investigated. (Nihmey, 1998, p. 163)

An investigation was held. A coroner's jury ruled in March of that year that the Hull police should offer compulsory courses to sensitize officers to the needs of visible minorities. However, despite that recommendation, four out of the five jurors felt that (personal) racism was not a factor in the case. The two statements seem to me to contradict each other. The fifth juror spoke out later to say that "We could have brought it up, not to accuse anybody, but to show there is racism" (Nihmey, 1998, p. 182). By the end of August 1990, the Quebec Police Commission cleared its officers of racism charges; they were deemed not to be "racially motivated" in their lack of full investigation of what had caused Minnie Sutherland to be barely conscious. Institutional racism does not seem to have been considered. There seems to have been no investigation of the actions of the Ottawa police, but there should have been.

Not the Police Alone: Contributing Factors

Of course, it was not the police alone that were the problem concerning the case. According to Nihmey, (1998, pp. 172–173) the media took the tack that Minnie was diabetic not drunk, aiming at the stereotype more than at the idea that she should have been treated with more respect even though she had been drinking, that being a "drunk Indian" was not her sole medical status. They too allowed the shadow of the stereotype to be cast over their view of the situation. This enabled the police to successfully defend themselves over an issue where they were in part right: she had been drinking. A half-truth trumps a total fiction.

Then there were the witnesses. Her cousin's testimony kept changing as she tried to figure out what actually happened, making it and her seem unreliable. And the nurse driver kept on insisting that Minnie had walked into the car, not that the car hit her. That would diminish the apparent seriousness of the injury, and would seem to play up the previous drinking.

The Drunk Tank

In a chapter on "Policing Winnipeg's Inner-City Communities," Comack writes about how "The Main Street Project," known informally as the drunk tank, was designed essentially as a location for supervised withdrawal from the effects of the abuse of alcohol and other drugs. Despite this formally designated purpose, it was used by the police as a place to dump Aboriginal people they had picked up for whatever reason, sometimes without testing that Aboriginal people were drunk. Where they were and when they were there was enough "evidence." In one example, a middle-aged Aboriginal woman was exiting a hotel. In her own words:

I was coming out of the side door and I almost, like, tripped but I was sober. I was just going to catch the bus and come back to the North End here…And just for that they just grabbed me and handcuffed me and said, "You are drunk." I said, "No. I haven't even been drinking, maybe one beer." But they still dragged me to the Main Street Project and I had to get in that cold little cell with just a blanket. (Comack, 2012, p. 175)

How Do You Dismantle a Stereotype?

Stereotypes, although seemingly simple, are often socially constructed of various parts. To dismantle or deconstruct or, to use a currently popular term, "unpack" a stereotype, you have to discover the constituent parts and deal with them one by one. One part of the stereotype of the "Indian drunk" is what can be called the **myth of biological helplessness.** This myth early on became an easy way to shift blame from the traders and big trading companies who were over-supplying alcohol to the people, from the governments and their officials who did little to stop or at least slow down the trade. A similar argument was made in the late nineteenth and early twentieth century that Aboriginal people were genetically predisposed to tuberculosis, when inferior government mandated reserve housing and residential schools were more to blame. In sociology this is known as **blame the victim,** and it often supplies great excuses for nothing to be done about a social problem.

The Anishinabe author George Copway saw the hypocrisy in this attitude and wrote about it in his nineteenth-century bestseller *The Traditional History and Characteristic Sketches of the Ojibway Nation,* first published in 1850. As he was trained as a minister, he used the language of religion to make the same point as I have been making, blaming white ministers as well as government officials (i.e., the "sluggards"):

The ministry of this country, and the sluggards in the cause of humanity, say now: There is a fate or certain doom on the Indians, therefore we need do nothing for them. How blasphemous! First you give us rum

> by the thousand barrels, and, before the presence of
> God and this enlightened world, point to God, and
> charge him as the murderer of the unfortunate Indi-
> ans. (Copway, 1972, pp. 264-265)

This stereotype in itself involves several ideas, including the
notion that Aboriginal people get drunk faster than other people (they do not), that they have no biological resistance to alcohol, so cannot drink in moderation (as if they were
natural-born alcoholics—also not true), that they cannot metabolize or process alcohol as well as non-Aboriginal people
can. The latter point has been discussed at great length and
has never been proven conclusively. An article probably most
often referred to in the literature, written by medical doctors
Lynn J. Bennion and Ting-Kai Li, entitled "Alcohol Metabolism in American Indians and Whites: Lack of Racial Differences in Metabolic Rate and Liver Alcohol Dehydrogenase,"
published in the *New England Journal of Medicine* in 1976,
involved the study of the rate of ethanol metabolism in 30
"American Indians" and 30 "Whites," along with biopsy spec-
imens of livers from seven of the former and six of the later.
The study concluded that it is "unlikely that alleged racial differences in response to alcohol can be explained on the basis
of racial differences in the rate of alcohol metabolism" (Bennion & Li, 1976, p. 9; see also Dyck, 1986). This faulty notion
of racial differences is seen in that way as a kind of analogy
with the 'White man's' diseases for which there were no prior
immunities.

There are a few statistics that take pieces out of the
stereotype. One is that a much higher percentage of the Aboriginal than the non-Aboriginal population of Canada completely abstain from drinking alcohol. This statistic has been
reported, among other places, in three separate studies of the
early 1990s in Canada, in the Aboriginal Peoples Survey, (Statistics Canada, 1993), the Yukon Alcohol and Drug Abuse
Survey (Yukon Government, 1991), and in nine northern Cree
communities in Quebec, (Santé Quebec, 1994). In the first
two studies, the Aboriginal population had about twice the abstinence rate of non-Aboriginal people studied. The first study
showed that fewer Aboriginal people drink alcohol daily or

weekly than non-Aboriginal people. This is consistent with my own experience. Most Aboriginal people I know do not drink alcohol.

It is important to see that the stereotype has biological determinism written all over it, when there could be social factors that would diminish the influence of such an idea. Richard W. Thatcher, a sociologist, in his densely written book *Fighting Firewater Fictions: Moving Beyond the Disease Model of Alcoholism in First Nations* (2004), looks at the culture of drinking among Aboriginal people, and refers to it as the **firewater complex**: "a specific set of abiding beliefs and behavioural norms organized around beverage alcohol consumption" (Thatcher, 2004, p. 3). He feels that in Aboriginal culture, the binge drinking or problem drinking, not alcoholism as conceived of as a disease that Aboriginal people are often inflicted by is what needs most to be overcome. He describes it in the following way:

> The "Indian binge" is social; it is an event announced by the use of the noun "party" as a verb. To "go drinking" is to get together with others and "party." Participants drink beyond the point of inebriation until all the liquor is gone and there is no case to replenish the supply. The binge-drinking style characteristically encompasses sex, affection, and extreme sentimentality, insults, anger, and rage. (Thatcher, 2004, pp. 20-21)

Thatcher feels that this pattern had developed from historically formed particular socio-economic circumstances, which, if changed, would also diminish the problem drinking, something he believes is insufficiently targeted by those interested in reducing drunkenness and violence in reserves. For him, the cause, the nature and the cure are primarily sociological, not psychological or biological. He is concerned that **medicalizing** Aboriginal drinking (i.e., turning into primarily a medical problem that requires treatment) makes it seem to be fundamentally a biological problem, a physical inevitability that individuals cannot avoid except by abstinence. He is concerned that this medicalizing, with treatment based on what he terms the disease concept of treatment or DCT, is that it reinforces the stereotype that Aboriginal people as individuals and as a "race" are somehow genetically or biologically predisposed to alcoholism, and to have that alcoholism automatically lead to violence.

Thatcher points out that the social, economic, and political leaders in Canada's Aboriginal population are typically not among the binge drinkers, emphasizing that those that who are bicultural (i.e., secure in both the Aboriginal and non-Aboriginal worlds within Canada) tend not to indulge in the problem drinking. The inevitability is not there.

Success Stories vs. Stereotypes

Demonstrating individual agency is another way of fighting or dismantling the stereotype, of denying the inevitability. Success stories of individuals and institutions, even those that follow what Thatcher would call the DCT, contribute in this way. They provide examples that counter the stereotypes. The following are stories of that type. It is interesting that all three stories, well known in the literature, all originated in the West (Alberta and British Columbia) in the early 1970s.

Alkali Lake

Alkali Lake is a community of the Shuswap or Secwepemc (a Salish-speaking people) of central British Columbia. The Salish-speaking peoples in Canada live in the south of the mainland of British Columbia and the east coast of Vancouver Island. The beginning of their alcohol story is a familiar one. The people were subjected to many forms of abuse at the nearby Williams Lake residential school, experiencing its devastating effects as late as the 1950s and the 1960s. Alcohol was one way of escaping the pain of that experience. Although alcohol could not be purchased legally on the reserve at that time, taxis and buses brought in a great supply. In addition, there was always the ready supply that came from local makers of rotgut homebrew. Drinking parties lasted several days. Women and children were beaten and raped. People died from alcohol and from alcohol-related incidents. Francis Johnson described the following recurring incident of his childhood:

> Many times our parents left us children alone when they went to town. When they went in the bar, we would spend hours waiting in the truck, not knowing when they would be back. Many times we went to bed hungry and without knowing when our parents would get back. (York, 1990, p. 178)

It should not be surprising, then, that the community was known in the area as "Alcohol Lake." Things seemed hopeless, the stereotype fulfilled.

In 1972, one family, the Chelseas, started the community of Alkali Lake back on the path to sobriety. Phyllis Chelsea had just arrived at her mother's to pick up her seven-year-old daughter but the girl refused to go, saying, "You and Daddy drink too much" (York, 1990, p. 179). Phyllis Chelsea poured her bottle of liquor down the sink, becoming sober from that day on, the first in her community to walk down that path. A strong sense of family would also help others, later, to walk that same path (Johnson & Johnson, 1993, p. 228-229).

A few months later, her husband Andrew joined her. The turnaround moment for him happened when he saw a group of children with bruised faces walking to school after their parents had been drinking all night. When he asked them whether they had had anything to eat that morning and they replied "no," he decided to stop drinking. The place on the road where he saw the children became sacred to him. He would revisit it to remind himself why he had quit drinking.

Andrew Chelsea was elected chief in 1973 and quickly took action against local bootleggers, arranging a sting operation with the local RCMP, and banning from the reserve a bus driver who made runs carrying thousands of dollars worth of alcohol. His wife became the welfare supervisor and arranged to have welfare cheques replaced with food and clothing vouchers. They had to fight local retailers for that gain. The next big step came from the community, which developed a supportive series of Alcoholics Anonymous-style "Alcoholism Awareness" meetings. When people went away to treatment centres, they received a constant flow of cards and letters of support. While they were away supportive members of the community painted and repaired their houses.

In 1985, more than 1,000 Native people and addiction counsellors from across Canada and the United States came to Alkali Lake to attend an international conference on alcohol abuse. That same year they made a video entitled *The Honour of All: The Alkali Lake Story*, which has since been used effectively to teach other Native communities that such a change is possible. By 1988, three quarters of the band members (in a community of over 400) had completed an alcohol treatment program. By 1989, more than 90 percent of band members were reported as being sober.

Spiritual traditions, here as in other places, played a very important role. When members of the community of Alkali Lake began their struggle against alcoholism, there was almost no practice of traditional spiritual ceremonies in the community. With the help of elders from other Shuswap communities, reviving spiritual practices such as the sweat lodge, sweetgrass, and pipe ceremonies played a key role in the rehabilitation of the community.

A 1992 study looking at the success of Alkali Lake's fight against alcohol, conducted by drug and alcohol counsellors Joyce and Fred Johnson, demonstrated the importance of spirituality in the recovery process. When the people were asked, "What significant event or thing caused you to want to be sober?" 31% responded, "spiritual support." When asked, "What have been the most effective factors in your after-care programs?" 34% answered, "spiritual support" (Johnson & Johnson, 1993, p. 229).

Nechi Institute

Another product of Aboriginal initiative against alcoholism in the early 1970s is the Nechi Institute, of northern Alberta, the name based on a Cree word for "friend." On October 15, 1974, it incorporated as a non-profit society to train addiction counsellors. It provided the first addictions diploma in Alberta. The institute believes that Aboriginal alcoholics and drugs abusers are best treated by Aboriginal counselors, using methods that reflect Aboriginal cultures, and that communities are best healed by Aboriginal-run programs. It has trained counsellors that work all across Aboriginal Canada.

Poundmaker's Lodge

Poundmaker's Lodge (now known as Poundmaker's Lodge Treatment Centres), named after a part Cree, but adopted Blackfoot leader of the late nineteenth century, was established near Edmonton in 1973, and it has developed an enviable record of accomplishment since that time. It offers a 90-day young adult program and a 42-day adult residence program, combining traditional beliefs and practices (e.g., pipe and smudge ceremonies and the sweat lodge) with more standard group therapy practices. It now takes non-Aboriginal as well as Aboriginal clients.

If you want to read a personal story that shows the good effect that Poundmaker's Lodge can have, read Herb Nabigon's *The Hollow Tree: Fighting Addiction with Traditional Native Healing* (2006). This story has particular resonance with me as I met the author as a colleague at Laurentian University. He became a classic case for me of what you see (at first) with an Aboriginal person, is not what you get. You can get much, much more. Herb Nabigon is Anishinabe (Ojibwa). Like with the story of Alkali Lake, the negative side of his story began with residential school, which he entered for the first time at nine years old. That painful dislocating experience led him to alcohol. Alcoholism took his right arm one drunken night when he was struck by a train. With several stops, he slowly pursued a career in social work at college and at university, but did not really seem to be going anywhere. The turning point in his life occurred when his Aboriginal employer pressed him into going to Poundmaker's Lodge. There he was exposed to the teachings of several Cree elders. They guided him to his second path of life, a more spiritual and sober one. Nabigon is now an Emeritus Professor, after teaching for many years in the Native Human Services program at Laurentian University in Sudbury, Ontario. His success story diminishes the stereotype.

Ted Nolan: The Power of a Stereotype[3]

Still, the stereotype can act against individual success. Ted Nolan (born 1958) is an Anishinabe from the Garden River First Nation near Sault Ste. Marie, Ontario. He played for three seasons in the NHL, coached in the minors, and then ended up as head coach for the Buffalo Sabres (from 1995 to 1997), eventually winning the coach of the year award. He was fired that same year (1997). From that time until 2006 to 2008, when he coached the New York Islanders, he did not coach in the NHL. He feels, rightly, I believe, that this has racist connotations. The general mainstream media line is that he had difficulties getting a coaching job as he was perceived to be a "GM (General Manager) killer," a handy label. He is currently (2012) coaching the Latvian men's national hockey team.

I believe that the stereotype of the Indian drunk helped to discredit him. He had a lot in his favour in terms of overcoming the stereotype. In 1986 he was chosen as a role model in the National Native Alcohol and Drug Abuse Program. He has been involved for over 20 years in working with Aboriginal youth (especially now through the Ted Nolan Foundation which, among others things provides a scholarship in the name of his mother, who was killed by a drunk driver), helping develop their leaderships abilities and wise lifestyle choices. In addition he helped fellow Anishinabe hockey player Chris Simon fight alcoholism. All of this did not free him from the stereotype of the Indian drunk. When he was still coaching in Buffalo, he missed a couple of practices, leaving the assistant coaches to run them, as sometimes happens throughout the league for team practices. The rumours began to spread that he had been drunk for three days, and that he had been drunk at some other practices. The rumours were false, but I suspect they are part of the reason why he has had a hard time finding an NHL coaching job.

Conclusions

Recall that with the J. J. Harper case, his master status of "Indian" overrode his middle-class economic position or status and his status of local political leader when he was spotted by a white police officer. In the case of Minnie Sutherland, the fact that she was an Indian who had been drinking meant that the stereotype of the "drunk Indian" overrode the other medical status as "victim of an accident" for the police officers she encountered on the night of her accident. They did not "see" the accident victim clearly because the stereotype stood in the way. Her death was more than just an "unfortunate incident"; it was one that was preventable but for the existence of the stereotype.

Lowering the Aboriginal problem with alcohol is a long-term goal that involves not just simplistic ways of dealing just with alcohol, but with economic and social problems, and of diminishing the stereotype that exists in many people's minds. In this chapter, the concern has been with the latter difficulty and its implications for policing.

We have seen that the stereotype of the Indian drunk was firmly established in Canada over the centuries, to a large extent the product of trading company practices and the all-encompassing power of the Indian Act. For many non-Aboriginal people, particularly those who live and visit the downtown areas of western Canadian cities, it is the first picture that comes to mind when the subject of Aboriginal people comes up. The stereotype has a long history of influencing how non-Aboriginal people, including the police, deal with Natives. It presents a major obstacle for policing services to overcome in their just treatment of Aboriginal citizens of their jurisdictions. Dismantling the stereotype and replacing it with a more balanced image presents a challenge that policing services, the education system, and the greater Canadian population generally need to and will overcome. Law professor Michal Jackson summed this type of situation up well in his 1987 publication, *Locking up Natives in Canada*, written for the conservative Canadian Bar Association:

> Those in criminal justice typically see native people at the worst part of their lives. Police, sheriffs, judges and prison staff don't see native communities and their leadership solving their own problems. They see the people who have failed. They rarely come into contact with the native leaders responding to problems in positive, effective ways. From that viewpoint, the response is predictable: "How clan native people do this [i.e., be effective leaders, productive individuals, or protection-worthy citizens] when they can't stand up straight?" (Jackson, 1987, as quoted in Comeau and Santin, 1990, p. 132)

Make an attempt to know the whole people, and hopefully the shadow of the Indian drunk stereotype will no longer be cast.

Questions

1. Stereotypes are readily reinforced by what can be called the **power of probability**. If you work as a police officer in western Canadian cities such as Winnipeg, Regina, Saskatoon, Calgary, Edmonton, or Vancouver, chances are that a significant number of Aboriginal people you will meet on a night patrol will be Aboriginal people who have been drinking, many of whom may have been drinking too much. If you want to be able to keep an open mind about those you encounter that may have not being drinking (or engaged in any illegal activity), or have only been drinking moderately, how do you keep the stereotype from controlling your interaction?

2. If you were a historian writing about or a teacher instructing students about Fort Whoop Up, how would you work to establish a more balanced picture of what went on?

3. If you were trying to convince someone of the untruth of the drunken Indian stereotype, what three points would you make first?

4. What could the first two officers have done that might have prevented Minnie's death?

5. What could the third officer have done that might have prevented Minnie's death?

6. If you were the police chief in a town or city where there were a significant number of Aboriginal people, what would you do to diminish the influence of the "drunk Indian" stereotype among your police officers?

7. What does it mean to say that non-drinking Aboriginal people are relatively "invisible" in the city?

8. What do you think the role of the stereotype of the Indian drunk had in keeping Ted Nolan from getting an NHL coaching job? Do you think that it was merely racism instead?

9. What are the pros and cons of a reserve banning alcohol, being "dry"?

Key terms

blame the victim–This term applies to a situation in which the person who is affected by some form of discrimination, unfair practice, or lack of decent opportunity is blamed for her or his situation. (See William Ryan, 1971, *Blaming the Victim*, New York: Pantheon.)

discretionary–This term is used to refer to the independent agency an official has regarding the justice system—to charge or not to charge for a police officer, to vary the length of a jail sentence for a judge.

firewater complex–"a specific set of abiding beliefs and behavioural norms organized around beverage alcohol consumption" (Thatcher, 2004, p. 3).

medicalizing–the process of turning a social or psychological problem into a medical one.

myth of biological helplessness–refers to the set of beliefs concerning Aboriginal inability to handle alcohol, to metabolize it, to drink and not act violently.

over-policing–refers to a situation in which the discretionary power of police officers is used consistently to overcharge or over-arrest or in other ways persecute a particular group.

paternalism–a way of treating people as if they were childhood, incapable of handling the basic responsibilities over their lives.

stereotype–an exaggerated but generally publicly accepted set of beliefs about a particular group, as if all members of the group participate equally in the (usually) negative aspects of the belief.

Notes

[1] In the Ojibwe language the term for alcohol is *shkadewaaboo*, with the *shkade* referring to fire and the *aaboo* referring to water (Rhodes, 1985, p. 617).

[2] For a discussion of this situation, in which the OPP shot and killed an unarmed man, Anishinabe Dudley George, at Ipperwash, Ontario in 1995, see Steckley & Cummins (2007, pp. 203-212).

³   In terms of hockey, there is another stereotype with respect to Aboriginal people, that of the Aboriginal enforcer.
This, too, limits their participation in the sport.

References

Bennion, L.J., & Ting-Kai L. (1976). Alcohol metabolism in
American Indians and Whites–Lack of racial differences
in metabolic rate and liver alcohol dehydrogenase. *New
England Journal of Medicine, 294*, 9-13.

Canadian Press. (2009, January 11). Home-brewed 'super-
juice' plagues Manitoba's north. *CTV News.* Retrieved
from http://www.ctv.ca/CTRVNews/Canada/20090111/
SUPER_juice_090111

Comack, E. (2012). *Racialized policing: Aboriginal People's
encounters with the police.* Halifax, NS: Fernwood Publishing.

Comeau, P., & Santin, A. (1990). *The First Canadians–A profile of Canada's Native people today.* Toronto, ON: James
Lorimer and Company.

Copway, G. (Kah-ge-ga-gah-bowh). (1972/1850). *The traditional history and characteristic sketches of the Ojibway.*
Toronto, ON: Coles Publishing Ltd.

Dyck, L. (1986). Are North American Indians biochemically
more susceptible to the effects of alcohol? *Native Studies
Review, 2*(2), 85-95.

Francis, D. (1992). *The imaginary Indian: The images of the
Indian in Canadian culture.* Vancouver, BC: Arsenal Pulp
Press.

Government of Yukon. (1991). *Yukon alcohol and drug survey*
(Vol. 1, Technical Report). Whitehorse, YT: Yukon Government Executive Council Office, Bureau of Statistics.

Jackson, M. (1989). *Locking up Natives in Canada.* Ottawa,
ON: Canadian Bar Association.

Johnson, J., & Johnson, F. (1993). Community development,
sobriety and after-care at Alkali Lake Band. In *the path
to healing: Report on the national round table on Aboriginal health and social issues.* Ottawa, ON: Royal Commission on Aboriginal Peoples.

Maracle, B. (1994). *Crazywater: Native voices on addiction
and recovery.* Toronto, ON: Penguin Books.

Nabigon, H. (2006). *The hollow tree: Fighting addiction with traditional Native healing.* Montreal, QC: McGill-Queen's University Press.

Nihmey, J. (1998). *Fireworks and folly: How we killed Minnie Sutherland.* Ottawa, ON: Phillip Diamond Books.

Pelletier, W., & Poole, T. (1973). *No foreign land: The biography of a North American Indian.* New York, NY: Pantheon Books.

Quigley, T. (1994). Some issues in sentencing of Aboriginal offenders. In Richard Gosse (Ed.), *Continuing Poundmaker's and Riel's quest: Presentations made at a conference on Aboriginal Peoples and justice.* Saskatoon, SK: Purich Publishing.

Rhodes, R. (1985). *Eastern Ojibwa-Chippewa-Ottawa dictionary.* Amsterdam: Mouton Publishing.

Rudin, J. (2007). *Aboriginal Peoples and the criminal justice system.* Ottawa, ON: Ontario Ministry of the Attorney General. Retrieved from http://www.attorneygeneral.jus.gov.on.ca

Santé Quebec. (1994). *A Health Profile of the Cree.* In Carole Daveluy & Lisa Bertrand (Eds.), *Report of the Santé Quebec Survey of the James Bay Area.* Montreal, QC: Santé Quebec.

Schmalz, P. (1991). *The Ojibwa of Southern Ontario.* Toronto, ON: University of Toronto Press.

Simard, C. (2010, March 27). Will a booze ban save the kids of Natuashish? *Winnipeg Free Press.* Retrieved from http://www.winnipegfreepress.com

Statistics Canada. (1993). *1991 Aboriginal Peoples survey: Language, Tradition, health, lifestyle and social issues* (Catalogue Number 89-533). Ottawa, ON: Ministry of Industry, Science and Technology.

Steckley, J., & Cummins, B. (2001). *Full circle: Canada's First Nations.* Toronto, ON: Pearson Canada.

Steckley, J., & Cummins, B. (2007). *Full circle: Canada's First Nations* (2nd ed.). Toronto, ON: Pearson Canada.

Stymeist, D. (1975). *Ethnics and Indians: Social relations in a northwestern Ontario town.* Toronto, ON: Peter Martin.

Thatcher, R.W. (2004). *Fighting firewater fictions: Moving beyond the disease model of alcoholism in First Nations.* Toronto, ON: University of Toronto Press.

Turner, J. (2011, March 27). The burden of proof. *Winnipeg Sun*. Retrieved from http://www.winnipegsun.com

Wadden, M. (2008). *Where the pavement ends: Canada's Aboriginal recovery movement and the urgent need for reconciliation*. Vancouver, BC: Douglas and McIntyre.

York, G. (1990). *The dispossessed: Life and death in Native Canada*. London: Vintage.

Chapter 5

The Neil Stonechild Case

In the words of Craig Neurf, former Saskatoon Police Service's Aboriginal liaison officer, "An Aboriginal kid in Saskatoon today stands a better chance of ending up in the criminal justice system than finishing high school" (Stackhouse, 2001).

Referring to 2003 statistics, authors Latimer and Foss (2004) note, "Aboriginal youth in Saskatchewan were thirty times more likely to be incarcerated than their non-Aboriginal counterparts" (as cited in Comack, 2012, p. 85).

Elizabeth Comack (2012) explains, "In Saskatchewan, Aboriginal people made up 11 percent of the population and a whopping 81 percent of provincial sentenced custody admissions in 2007-8" (pp. 84-85).

In 2001, Jim Madden, the mayor of Saskatoon, and a former police officer, remarked, "You have a segment of the population afraid of the police...and a segment of the police afraid of the population" (Stackhouse, 2001).

And, concerning starlight tours, Mayor Madden replied in the following way to a reporter's questions: "It's happened. Should it happen? I don't think so. Will it happen again? I would hope not" (Stackhouse, 2001). That did not give the people much hope.

Introduction: Starlight Tours

Starlight tours involve the questionable practice of police officers driving people under the influence of alcohol or other drugs outside or on the outskirts of town, so that they have to walk back to where they want and need to be. It may have first developed in warm places, where the dangers of exposure or hypothermia were slight. That is not the case in Saskatoon for much of the year. In Saskatoon, the only recorded instances or even suspicions of instances that I have ever read about are with Aboriginal people. The practice is not, of course, unique to the Saskatoon police (see Comack, 2012, pp. 181-186); it is just that the Saskatoon cases made the headlines, especially when death occurred.

In 1997, Brian Trainor, a veteran police officer, wrote a column entitled "Tales from the Blue Lagoon" for the weekly newspaper the *Saskatoon Sun* that told a story about one night on the beat for two "fictional" officers, "Hawk" and "Gumby." In the story, they pick up a loud, abusive Aboriginal drunk person and take him on a starlight tour, driving him outside of the city of Saskatoon. The column ended as follows:

> Sensing that this wasn't the way home, the drunk began to demand he be taken to the highest power in the land. A few quick turns and the car comes to an abrupt stop in front of the Queen Elizabeth II Power Station. Climbing out and opening the rear door, he yelled for the man to get out, advising him that this was the place he had asked to go to. Quickly gathering his wits, the drunk tumbled out of the car and into the thickets along the riverbank, disappearing from view. One less guest for breakfast. (Trainor 1997, as cited in Kossick, 2000)

This is not just fiction. It has been happening for real. The earliest recorded instance of this happening in the city of Saskatoon was in 1976. On May 22 of that year, three Aboriginal people, two men and a woman who was eight months pregnant, all of whom had been drinking, were taken by police beyond the city limits of Saskatoon and left there to take a long walk back home. Almost five months later, the police officer involved was charged with breaches of discipline, a charge that came with a $200 fine. Whether the practice continued for the years immediately following that is not officially recorded. What follows are more recent cases.

Rodney Naistus

On January 27, 2000, a starlight tour would take a deadly turn. Rodney Naistus, a 25-year-old Cree man from the Onion Lake reserve had just been released from Saskatoon's Correctional Centre's Urban Camp facility. His long-term plan for after his release was to travel back to the reserve with one of his male cousins, to live there in their grandfather's house. His short-term plan was to celebrate his release with family and friends. According to his cousin Charlene, at whose house in Saskatoon they were having a few drinks, Rodney "was just so happy. We were all partying with him. We were just celebrating that he was there with us" (McNairn, 2004).

Naistus decided he would go from his cousin's house with a friend, against the advice of Charlene and others, to a local nightclub. That was the last time they would see him alive. His body was found on Saturday, January 29 in the Holiday Park industrial area, a short distance away from the power station, the "highest power" in the land of the fictional story.

Lawrence Kim Wegner

On the night of January 30, 2000, Lawrence Kim Wegner, a popular 30-year-old Cree freshman social work student at the Saskatchewan Indian Federated College went on a drug binge with his roommates. He left their shared apartment between 8:00 and 10:00 p.m., after shooting up a mixture of morphine and synthetic cocaine. The young man who left with him had collapsed within an hour of leaving the apartment and was taken by his family to a hospital. Sometime between 11 o'clock and midnight, Wegner showed up banging on the door of the apartment of some distant relatives of his, yelling "Pizza, pizza." Not recognizing who he was, one of the relatives called the police, only to be informed that someone else had called about Wegner sooner.

At some later point, Wegner was arrested and driven outside the city. His autopsy revealed that he had a large bruise (six by four centimetres) above his left eye, haemorrhaging under his scalp with small abrasions on his hands and left forearm, but it was ruled later that there was "no external evidence of gross violence or trauma to the body" (Reber &

Renaud, 2005, p. 161). In the inquest that followed, it was revealed that a passerby, an army veteran, said that he was out driving near midnight that night and observed two police officers shoving a man matching Wegner's description into the back of their cruiser. Wegner's body was not discovered until February 3, 2000, in a wheat-stubble field by the power station, apparent evidence for another starlight tour.

Darrell Night's Story About his Starlight Tour

An apparent survivor story was reported to the police shortly after these two cases came to light. Darrell Night, a Cree, and a friend of Rodney Naistus told the story that from the night of January 27 to early morning on January 28, 2000, the big, sturdy 33-year-old unemployed bricklayer got drunk. He had a criminal record, for fights when drunk, and stood tall at six feet, three inches and weighed heavy at 240 to 260 pounds. At some point during the night, he saw two officers in a police car. According to the officers, he lunged at their vehicle, flashed an obscene gesture at them, swore, and hit their car with his hand. They then arrested him for causing a disturbance, handcuffed him, and put him in the vehicle. Then, according to Night, rather than driving him to the police station to charge him, they turned to drive him out into the country, specifically to the Queen Elizabeth II Power Station south of the city.

This would have put him into an extremely dangerous situation. The temperature was about minus 22 degrees Celsius, and he was not wearing a coat, just a denim jacket. Abandoned by the police, and quite aware of the danger of his situation, Night then walked over to the power station and was able to get a night watchman to call him a cab. Doing that may have saved his life from death by exposure.

Night did not relate his story to anyone in legal authority for a while. After all, he was Aboriginal and the police officers were white. Who would the authorities most likely believe? His claim was that he would later come forward with his information once he heard about other similar stories relating to other Aboriginal men. The story of the two officers at the time was that he had asked to be dropped off. They would stick with that story.

One Spin of the Story in the Conservative Press

The conservative press has come to challenge this story with "new evidence" since the inquiry discussed below into the death of Neil Stonechild. Candis McLean, a writer for the ultra-conservative and anti-Aboriginal publication *Western Standard* (read any of their issues, particularly Mclean's writing, and this skewed perspective will soon come across), wrote an article on April 12, 2004, entitled "Rush to Judgment" in which she portrayed to two police officers who were charged in his case, Ken Munson and Dan Hatchen, as innocent victims and the RCMP investigators as incompetent. She would later do the same regarding the Neil Stonechild case. She built her argument around the presence of one of Night's cousins who lived only about two and a half kilometres away from where he was dropped off. After writing the article, she later made a documentary, *When Police Become Prey*, which was first shown in March of 2007 to further spread her story. You can see in her work that she feels that **political correctness** had gone wild in this case, that Aboriginal people were being given automatic privilege by the legal system (as represented by the RCMP) over local white police officers. The term political correctness has to be contextualized before we move on in this discussion.

Political Correctness

The term political correctness is typically used to refer to the generally well-intentioned, if sometimes misguided, attempts to limit speech and writing by censoring words, and to restrict practices that exhibit and promote racism, sexism, classism, ablism, and other forms of discrimination (see Steckley & Letts, 2010, pp. 257-258). The term is used and perceived in two different ways depending on the social location and biases of the user. For people who are victims of the discrimination, and to those who are sympathetic to such victims, the actions related to political correctness are used to promote respect and justice for those who are discriminated against. For those individuals who are members of the dominant society–typically white, male, middle class and conservative–the term is used as a conversation, discussion and thinking stopper. "That is just political correctness" is as dismissive as saying, "that meat is rotten; we can't eat it," or, "it is raining outside; we can't go outside to play baseball." It comes with an automatic assumption that "liberal institutions" are discriminating in favour of undeserving minorities at the expense of the deserving majority or dominant population, and "special interests" are controlling politics. Remember that all interest groups, such as oil companies, drug companis, religions and unions, powerful and non-powerful, are special interest groups. When such people see what they believe is "special treatment" of minority groups to which they do not belong, they often invoke the word as if it were a magic charm giving them permission to think no further. If the weapon of political incorrectness is not pointed at you, it is hard to know how it wounds. It is as unthinking as its opposite, as believing that Aboriginal people are always right and white police officers are always wrong when there is a conflict between the two. Both extremes are simply wrong.

Right wing, conservative media are often involved in crusades in which they automatically side with the police, and against Aboriginal people, responding to perceived bias in what they believe is the "liberal media" by piling up bias on their own side, quoting only or almost exclusively police and police-sympathetic sources. To get at journalistic "truth" you have to look at both sides of the argument and determine from the situation who is more in the right and who is more in the wrong. There are at least as many conservative media voices (*The Sun*, and the *National Post*, for example) as there are liberal ones.

McLean's use of "Native Indian" in her article to refer to one of the victims of the starlight tours tells a lot about her perspective. The term would be deemed politically incorrect. It does not identify his nation, which is like calling a German merely "some European dude" or "some sausage-eating white guy." Use of the technically incorrect "Indian" also lacks respect, as it is considered an insult by many Aboriginal people. The word can be used in joking ways between Aboriginal people, like the n-word can be among black people. There is no equal expression for white people, but as they are the dominant majority in Canadian society, that should not be surprising. The powerful generally have few negative names attached to them. While use of a respectful term does not always indicate a positive attitude (i.e., the individual could just be giving the appearance of respect), use of a disrespectful term is a good indicator of a deeper negative attitude.

It should be noted that there is also another documentary that has been produced about the Darrell Night case. It is entitled *Two Worlds Colliding*. Tasha Hubbard is the writer/director, Bonnie Thompson the producer, and it is done by the National Film Board of Canada. I would recommend it.

The Investigation

To their credit, the Saskatoon Police Service (SPS) began investigating the matter right after Darrell Night's complaint. They would confine their investigation to the Night case. No one has ever been charged with the deaths of Naistus and Wegner. The next week, two veteran officers involved with Night's starlight tour were suspended with pay. Then police chief of the SPS, Dave Scott, stated that he took this action in order to maintain public trust and the trust of the Aboriginal community (something that was unlikely to have existed to any great extent at that time). Still, he also said that he did not believe that the officers suspended were connected in any way with the deaths of Naistus and Wegner. Scott was quoted as saying:

> Is this widespread? Are there reasons for me, as chief, to be concerned about the activities of our police officers? At this time I have no indication of that…I would ask first that you have confidence in me as the chief of police and the leader of this police service, to ensure that a complete investigation will be done properly and I can assure you it will be. (Zakreski, 2000)

On February 16, the RCMP took over the investigation with a special task force of 16 RCMP officers (not including support staff), making it the largest investigative unit it had ever deployed in Saskatchewan. By March 10, the Saskatoon Police Commission suspended without pay the officers who admitted to dropping off Night. The Saskatoon Police

Association protested this action. In the words of its president, Al Stickney, "They're on their own. These are two guys with families and no paycheque, who have not been convicted of any wrongdoing" (Perreaux, 2000).

Retired Aboriginal police officer Oliver Williams adds another piece to this story, one otherwise overlooked by the police. In attempt to make sure the case was handled fairly, Williams came out of retirement to oversee the proceedings:

> Not trusting the RCMP to do a clean investigation, Oliver Williams, a Native police officer, comes out of retirement to oversee the proceedings. He is aware of the situation, and, to gather more information, he sets up a call line. In a short time, he receives over 800 calls outlining abuses in the system. He states that, as a policeman, he is ashamed; as a citizen, he is appalled, and, as an Aboriginal, he is angry. (Loreto, 2007)

Even granted that some of the claims will be exaggerations, possibly even made up, this is a very significant response.

About a month after their suspension without pay, the two officers were charged with "unlawful confinement and assault." Reber and Renaud described the officers' testimony in the following telling way:

> From the beginning, they did not dispute leaving the native man near the power plant on the night in question, but to them they hadn't committed a crime, merely an error in judgment. Both officers said they were ashamed of what they had done, but claimed they were only doing as Night had asked. (Reber & Renaud, 2005, p. 256)

Eventually, an all white jury convicted them of unlawful confinement, but declared them innocent of assault. They were fired immediately.

On October 31, 2001, it was announced that the two officers had asked for a sentencing circle. **Sentencing circles** are alternatives to jail time. These are available in some parts of Canada to convicted Aboriginal people, and they have all the players in the offence, including the families of the victims, involved in the circle. There are no judges. Everyone gets to speak; apologies can and often are given. The form that the sentencing takes is agreed upon by the people in the circle. The sentencing circles are based on traditional Aboriginal notions of restorative rather than punitive justice, and they have diminished the number of Aboriginal people doing jail time.

A few days later, in an article in the *Globe and Mail*, John Stackhouse described the officers' request for a sentencing circle as "so bizarre that it prompted laughter in the courtroom and anger on the part of natives, who felt they were being mocked" (Stackhouse, 2001, p. F2). Understandably, their request was denied. They were sentenced to eight months jail time, but served only four. In March 2003, their conviction was upheld. An appeal was later denied.

Lloyd Joseph Dustyhorn and D'arcy Dean Ironchild

Two other deaths of Aboriginal men that happened early in 2000 are often linked to the starlight tour deaths. One is that of Lloyd Joseph Dustyhorn, a 53-year-old man who was picked up for public intoxication in the evening of January 18. After spending some time "under observation" in a holding cell, he was driven home by a police officer early in the morning of January 19, and left on the doorstep or stoop of his home. He never made it inside. Dressed only in what can be called summer clothing, jeans, a shirt, boots and sock, he froze to death. The inquest into this death was held in May 8 to May 10, 2001. The jury concluded that his death was accidental and that it was due to hypothermia. They recommended the establishment in Saskatoon of an emergency detoxification centre as a place to temporarily house non-violent intoxicated and drugged individuals.

D'arcy Dean Ironchild was 33. He, too, was picked up for public intoxication, although the most potent substance he had abused that night was chloral hydrate, the combination with alcohol famously known as a Mickey Finn. Although there were some signs that he was hallucinating in the cell, he was sent home in a taxi. He died inside his home of a drug overdose. The inquest into his death, like that of Dustyhorn, ruled that death was accidental.

Neil Stonechild's Last Lonely Night

Neil Stonechild was the son of Stella Stonechild, a Saulteaux woman from Manitoba who had five children. Her first child Dean, was taken from her during what is called the Sixties Scoop, when, from the 1960s to the early 1980s, thousands of Aboriginal children were taken from their families, especially single-parent families such as that headed by Stella, and adopted out of their community, province (most were from Manitoba), and sometimes country. Dean, renamed Chris by his adoptive white American parents, was one of those shipped out of the country. Neil Stonechild was the second youngest child, born in 1973, with Erica (1969) and Marcel (1971) as his older siblings and Jake (1975) as his younger brother.

Neil must have known about starlight tours, as his younger brother Jake, at age 11, had endured what could be called a mini-starlight tour twice in one summer–with the police dropping him off out of town in warm weather, once even driving him to a bridge crossing the South Saskatchewan River and asking him whether he wanted to swim home (Reber & Renaud, 2005, p. 21).

Neil was no innocent. In 1990, he was serving a six-month open-custody in a community home. His offences were largely petty crimes, breaking car windows to steal the radios to sell for money for alcohol, and violating probation. He drank, but had got into few fights. He had spent time in the tough Kilburn Hall youth detention centre, so he was having an easier time of it at the less oppressive community home. His life wasn't all bad news. He was close to his family. He had succeeded in competitive wrestling, having once won the rookie of the year award for his wrestling club. Although he had quit the club, he was thinking of returning. He was also passing at school.

On November 24, 1990, he was deemed "unlawfully at large," as he had run away from his community home, cut school, but was staying with his mother and siblings. It was Saturday, and he wanted one last weekend of freedom. At 7:30 that night, he called the woman who ran the community home, and said that he would return on Sunday.

Neil Stonechild, wanting one last night's fun before his return to the community home, and his 16-year old friend Jason Roy were at a vodka and cards party with friends when he decided to see Lucille, his former girlfriend. Knowing that she was with her boyfriend at her sister Claudine's place babysitting her sister's children, he and Jason Roy headed out to see her. But first they went to a local 7-Eleven, which was filled with teenagers. Quietly, they took a few snacks and drinks, but, being somewhat drunk and filled with energy, they started pushing each other, knocking over some articles in the aisles. Hearing a voice yell at them from the counter, they decided to leave before they were identified. As it turns out, Neil was identified, and someone from the 7-Eleven called in his name to the police.

As they headed to Claudine's place, the two friends got separated. Not seeing any last names he knew to get him buzzed into the apartment building, Neil pressed many buttons, and was let in. Not knowing what door to knock on, Neil banged on all doors, until he got the right door but the wrong person. Claudine's white boyfriend, who was not in a good mood, answered the door, only to shut it again. Finding out from Lucille who it was, he called the police. There were now three reasons why the police would be looking for Neil Stonechild.

Constables Larry Hartwig and Bradley Senger arrived near the scene at about midnight.
They initially pull over Neil's cousin Bruce Genaille thinking it was him; the two look a lot alike. They told him his cousin was wanted for the disturbance at the 7-Eleven. Shortly afterwards, a key and contested part of the story takes place.

Jason Roy was returning on his own to the place where the party had been. A police cruiser surged ahead of him, leaving the road to block his path along the sidewalk. According to his later testimony, Jason saw Neil with a bloody face, and, based on his restricted body movements, he appeared to be restrained by handcuffs. He would later claim that Neil said that the police were going to kill him. Officers Hartwig and Senger asked Jason whether he knew Neil. Not wanting to be in that police cruiser himself, Jason understandably said that he did not know his friend. They then asked him his name, and he gave the name of his cousin Tracy Lee Horse. They allow him to leave.

The next day, Stella and the woman who ran the community home both expected to see or hear from him, but nothing was seen or heard of the young man. This went on for several days. Then, on Thursday, November 29, Neil Stonechild's body was found on the outskirts of town, his head in the snow. The police identification team noticed a few peculiarities. He was only wearing a sock on his right foot, no shoe. The sock showed signs that he had been walking on it. His left shoe was undone, and when it was removed a stone was found inside it. This is consistent with his having walked some distance on two sock feet before he was able to put one shoe on. In addition, there were two parallel deep scratches running horizontally across the bridge of his nose, and there was a cut on his lower lip. They did not call the crime lab to further investigate, as none of these injuries would have been sufficient to have caused his death. Strangely, they did not treat the place as a crime scene. They did not even look for his missing shoe. It was never found.

The investigator assigned to the case was British-born Sergeant Keith Jarvis of the Morality Section of the Saskatoon Police Services, a veteran of 24 years on the force. The case was left with the Morality Section as it was not an obvious homicide, in which situation it would have gone to Major Crimes. The case was handled badly right from the start.

When Jason Roy found out about his friend's death from the television news, he called the police, even though he knew it might put him in a compromised position, and, with his distrust of the police, he no doubt believed that it could lead to his arrest. He arranged to meet with Jarvis. Jason told Jarvis about seeing his friend in the back of the police vehicle, but this was not recorded in any of the investigator's notes, and the meeting was not taped. Jarvis said that he would look into it and get back to it. He did not.

Jarvis concocted his own theory as to what happened to Neil Stonechild. He came up with the idea that Neil was headed for the very tough and strict adult Correction Centre to turn himself in. There was no evidence for this, and is not likely that Neil would want to show up there. It would not make good sense for him to do so.

Jarvis worked on the case for two days, November 29 and 30, then took four days off and returned to it on December 5. He had urged Major Crimes to take over the case when he left, but found out on his return that they had done nothing. His written statements for the case did not contain much that could have been important. In addition to not reporting what Jason Roy said, he made no mention of discussing the case with Hartwig or Senger, who had been dispatched to find him. Reber and Renaud also list some other aspects of negligence on his part:

> He did not visit the site where Neil had died, missed the autopsy and inspected neither the body nor the still photographs Morton had taken. He didn't look at Neil's clothing or send it to be analyzed. His notes show he made a single attempt to locate the only suspect named in the investigation reports, Gary Pratt. (Reber & Renaud, 2005, p. 76)

On December 6, 1990, after officially closing the case, Jarvis called Stella Stonechild. He told her that his investigation had determined that there was no foul play. He stated his largely unfounded belief that her son had simply wandered about after drinking too much, headed towards the Correction Centre, fallen down and died from hypothermia—a purely accidental death. He promised that he would keep her informed if any new evidence arose. He never kept that promise.

Indian Ernie Enters the Scene

Ernie Louttit, a Cree man, joined the Saskatoon Police Service after serving in the army. He is a big man, over six feet tall. His personal policing style is to walk rather than to drive his beat. He has a certain amount of credibility with the Native youth, although some think that he has "sold out to the white man." He is known as "Indian Ernie" on the street.

Louttit knew the Stonechild boys, Neil and Jake, and even called Stella "mum." One day shortly after the news of Neil's death, he went to talk to Jake in an arcade, who told him what he knew and thought about the case. The next day Louttit made a copy of the closed case file. He was shocked and surprised that it had been closed so soon and with so little investigation, although he knew well how Aboriginal people were often treated differently as victims and suspects than other people were.

He was concerned by how short the investigation had been, so he went to talk to the police in Major Crimes, who dismissed him quickly as being only a beat cop. He then went to Stella, risking discipline by talking about his concerns about the case with her. By the end of 1990, he had written up his own thoughts on the case and took them to the head of Major Crimes, who, in turn, told him to take his ideas to Jarvis. He ended up pretty much in a shouting match with Jarvis, who accused him of meddling with a case that wasn't his, and threatened him with discipline if he took his concerns any farther.

He was not the only officer who had concerns at the time. A white officer, who knew the Stonechild family from church and from a friendship between Neil and one of his sons, also spoke with Stella, and took his concerns to Jarvis. He was shut down as well.

The last that would be heard for a long time on the case was when experienced journalist Terry Craig of the Saskatoon paper the *Star Phoenix* picked up on the case. He too spoke with Stella Stonechild and heard her concerns. Craig spoke with media relations officer Sergeant Dave Scott, who would later become chief of the SPS, who falsely claimed, with true public relations spin that "a tremendous amount of work went into that case" (as cited in Reber & Renaud, 2005, p. 95). Craig's article was published on March 4, 1991, under the title "Family Suspects Foul Play."

The police did not reopen the case. And, what seems strange to me, even Native leaders and organizations did not seem to take up the fight.

The Neil Stonechild Case Resurfaces

With all the publicity of the starlight tour cases, it would only be a matter of time before some journalist would do a little digging to find out whether this had ever happened before. That journalist would be Leslie Perreaux, not surprisingly, working for the *Star Phoenix*. He found Craig's article, talked with Neil's family, and published an article on February

22, 2000 with the major headline, "Decade-old Death Resurfaces," underneath which was the minor headline, "Neil Stonechild's family questions why he froze to death in this field" (as cited in Reber & Renaud, 2005, p. 186). The case was back in the public eye.

The SPS made moves to initiate an investigation, but the Saskatchewan minister of justice decided that it would be more appropriate for the RCMP to handle the situation. This in a number of ways set the two forces against each other, with the SPS engaging in a "shadow investigation" with its own investigators and outside experts, as if the two were on the opposite sides as prosecution and defence.

RCMP Superintendent Darrell McFadyen headed up the investigation, with Sergeant Ken Lyons leading up the work to be done. One of the first obstacles they would encounter in their work would be that Jarvis's official notes on the case had been destroyed. Fortunately, Ernie Louttit had kept his photocopied version so they could proceed more smoothly with the case.

The RCMP investigative work led to the public inquiry into Neil Stonechild's death that began on September 8, 2003. After months of testimony and legal argumentation, the final report was released on October 26, 2004. The inquiry arrived at 13 conclusions. First and second, it was clearly established that there were two complaints issued of Neil Stonechild causing a disturbance, and the Constables Bradley Senger and Larry Hartwig had been dispatched a little before midnight to investigate. The third and fourth were key; they indicated that the officers encountered Neil Stonechild and took him into custody, which the officers continued to deny. The fifth and sixth conclusions were relatively uncontroversial, saying that Stonechild died of exposure and that his frozen body had been found on November 29.

The seventh conclusion was, however, more controversial and damning. It stated that "there were injuries and marks on Stonechild's body that were liked caused by handcuffs." The RCMP's expert witness suggested that the marks on the wrists and across the nose were of the same dimensions. The SPS expert disagreed, arguing that the injuries came from walking through bushes or falling on frozen vegetation.

The eighth conclusion noted that the preliminary investigation set out by the SPS had "properly identified a number of suspicious circumstances surrounding the death." This was followed, however, by a damning indictment of Jarvis's work, that he had "carried out a superficial and totally inadequate investigation" of Stonechild's death. This included the tenth conclusion that he had not recorded the "important information" given to him by Jason Roy. And further, in the eleventh conclusion, Jarvis and his superior had not answered "the many questions that surrounded the Stonechild disappearance and death." The twelfth conclusion was Jarvis had dismissed "important information" that was given to him by two members of the SPS, Ernie Louttit, and his white colleague (p. 212 of the report, as quoted in Reber & Renaud, 2005, p. 384).

In the final conclusion, the report writer condemned how the SPS leadership had dealt with the case from 1990 onwards:

> In the years that followed, the chiefs and deputy chiefs of police who successively headed the Saskatoon Police Service rejected or ignored reports from the Stonechild family members and investigative reporters of the Saskatoon Star Phoenix that cast serious doubts on the conduct of the Stonechild investigation. The self-protective and defensive attitudes exhibited by the senior levels of the police service continued notwithstanding the establishment of an RCMP task force to investigate the suspicious deaths of a number of aboriginal persons and the abduction of an aboriginal man. These same attitudes were manifested by certain members of the Saskatoon Police Service during the inquiry. (p. 212, as quoted in Reber & Renaud, 2005, pp. 385-386)

On the day of the locally televised release of the inquiry report, Chief Russell Sabo of the SPS suspended constables Hartwig and Senger. On November 12, 2004, they were fired. It should be noted that the firing notices did not allege that they had driven Neil Stonechild to the isolated location, causing him to freeze to death, but instead charging them with failing to follow proper procedures in not recording that they had Stonechild in their custody, failing to process him properly and diligently, and failing to inform the appropriate personnel about having him in their custody during the inquiry that began in 2000. At the same time, the deputy chief who had been the SPS's point man in dealing with the inquiry was given two notices of formal discipline for issuing misleading statements to the media and for dishonourable conduct.

An arbitration hearing began in May 2005 to see whether the firing of the two officers was justified, and in March of 2006, the local police association applied to the Saskatchewan Court of Appeal to quash (i.e., set aside by judicial action) findings from the inquiry suggesting that the two officers had performed their duties improperly. The firing was upheld in 2008 by a three-member police commission panel.

The Social Context

It is important to study the social context in which the starlight tours occurred. It is not enough to accuse individuals of racism or negligence. That way does not create a solid understanding of why it happened, and how the situation can be improved. Certain conditions are more likely or more likely to cause such practices to take place. The following are some of the key factors involved.

Saskatoon's Rapidly Growing Aboriginal Population

In James Frideres' most recent (2012) authoritative book on Aboriginal people in Canada, he provides statistics for the growth of the Aboriginal population in Saskatoon over the 55-year period of 1951 to 2006. In 1951, there were 48 Aboriginals. Twenty years later, there were 1,070. Forty years after that (2001), there were 20,275. In 2006, the Aboriginal population grew to 2006, amounting to roughly 9.3% of the city's population. During the same period, the Aboriginal population in the city of Regina grew from 160 to 17,105. Similarly, there were spectacular growth levels in Winnipeg, Calgary, and Winnipeg.

In Saskatoon, and in the other Prairie cities, the figures show huge growth in the urban Aboriginal population, with the fastest growth occurring over the 25-year period from

1971 to 1996, the time period in which the Neil Stonechild case took place. It is reasonably safe to assume that the Aboriginal numbers are lower than actual, as this is generally the case in urban centres in Canada. For example, Frideres notes that the combined total (single Aboriginal origin and multiple origin including Aboriginal) population of Saskatoon was 22,165 in the 1991 census (2001, p. 148). I suspect that the Aboriginal population of Saskatoon, when First Nations and Métis are considered, would be close to 30,000, upping the percentage to about 15%.

Underrepresented and Equally Represented

In 1992, the Saskatchewan Indian Justice Review Committee reported that, despite the commitment to increase the complement of Aboriginal staff, less than 1% of police officers in Saskatoon were Aboriginal. The percentage has increased since then. Stackhouse (2001) claimed that 18 of the 94 constables hired from 1996 to 2001 were Aboriginal. The figures for December 31, 2006 reveal that this particular pattern of hiring process has continued.

Table 5.1 shows that the number of constables, at 11.8% is over the 9.3% of the officially recognized Aboriginal population percentage (but probably under the actual percentage), and the number of staff generally, at 8.9%, is slightly under the Aboriginal percentage.

Need for a Detox Centre

While it is not a good excuse for starlight tours, one reason why some Saskatoon police officers may have opted for that hard choice was the lack of a detoxification centre or detox centre in Saskatoon. When John Stackhouse wrote his *Globe and Mail* article "Welcome to Harlem on the Prairies" in 2001, he remarked that, despite efforts by Aboriginal groups and the Saskatoon Police Service to have such a centre, none existed in the city, unlike every other major city in the Prairie provinces. Instead, the only options the police had the "drunk tank" (i.e., jail) for most, but the emergency ward in local hospitals for the most intoxicated, a practice that is both very expensive and disruptive in the hospital. It was not until

Table 5.1
Winnipeg Police Service (WPS) Staffing by "Race" from 1997 to 2009

Occupational Groups	Total	Aboriginal Employees			
		Female	Male	Total	Percentage
Executive[1]	15	0	0	0	0
Supervisors[2]	107	2	4	6	5.6%
Constables	272	5	27	32	11.8%
Special Constables	51	3	0	3	5.9%
Civilian	15	0	0	0	0
Total	460	10	31	41	8.9%

Source: Saskatoon Police Service (2007).
Notes:
[1]   This number includes chief, deputy chiefs, superintendents, inspectors, and directors.
[2]   This number includes staff sergeants and sergeants.

2004 that such a detox centre, a brief detoxification unit was developed, with only a 12-bed capacity. Among the employees of this centre is one Aboriginal support worker. The need for expansion is probably rather high.

What Have You Done For/To Us Lately?

Aboriginal Liaison Officer

One of the first efforts put forward by the SPS to address their lack of close relationship with the Aboriginal population in and around Saskatoon took place in 1994, when they created the position of Aboriginal Liaison Officer. The Aboriginal organizations that were first approached concerning working with the person holding this position were the Saskatoon Tribal Council, the Federation of Saskatchewan Indian Nations, and the Métis Nation of Saskatchewan. The creation of this position was one major reason why, in 1995, the SPS won the national Ivan Ahenakew Award (named after an accomplished Saskatchewan Cree individual), which is "given to any business, company, government department or Aboriginal organization that has shown results in the areas of Recruitment and Training of Aboriginal personnel for employment and training for the current year" (IANE Inc).

Constable Mike McLean: A Positive View of an Aboriginal SPS Officer

In August 2008, in *Eagle Feather News*, Constable Mike McLean wrote an article about his work with the Saskatoon Police Service. He was the first Treaty Indian to occupy that position. He focused mainly on his three and a half years working as the Aboriginal liaison officer (ALO) for the SPS. He is Cree, raised on the James Smith Reserve, about 60 kilometres east of Prince Albert and a little more than twice that distance northeast of Saskatoon.

McLean was in his late thirties when he took advantage of an opportunity to become a police officer in the SPS. His prior experience was operating a small coffee shop in Saskatoon, after working in Vancouver over a long period of time.

After a short period as a patrol officer, he was offered the position as ALO. He worked with two others, non-Aboriginal people, in the Aboriginal Liaison Unit. His work involved developing partnerships with Aboriginal organizations in and around the Saskatoon area, and in making presentations to various groups. In his words:

> Our presentations involved instructing why diversity is important in a workplace, what it means to be tolerant of other races and cultures, and how people of different cultures and backgrounds add value to the communities. (McLean 2008, p. 17)

He believes that the biggest lesson he learned from his time in this position is "that people can be provided with the tools that they need but the changes of attitude must come from within" (McLean, 2008, p. 17). He feels that he has not experienced any (personal) racism at work, and he encourages other Aboriginal people to join the force.

During the first years of the twenty-first century, the SPS became involved with a number of programs that attempt to bridge the distance between the police and the Aboriginal population of Saskatoon. With the Department of Sociology at the University of Saskatchewan, the Aboriginal Justice and Criminology Program, they have been involved with a practicum (originally nine weeks, now it is one of several similar 12-week practicums) that place "students on a police shift with officers rotating through various units. The students obtain first-hand knowledge of the Police Service and police duties" (Sociology Department, University of Saskatchewan). Upon completion of the practicum, participants are required to develop a constructive critique of what they experience.

As youth were the main target for a more positive relationship between police and Aboriginal people, one early development was the Peacemaker program, which put at-risk Aboriginal youth, many directed through diversion from prison strategies to the program through the Saskatoon Tribal Council, and officers together. According to the SPS website, the purpose of the Peacemaker program was to

> allow youth to better understand negative behavior, the law and to develop positive relationships with police. These programs also serve a purpose for the Saskatoon Police Service, as outlined in the mandate of the Aboriginal Liaison position, to break down barriers that not only exist on the Aboriginal side, but on the police service side. (Saskatoon Police Service, Peacekeepers Program)

Programs included officer and youth participation in sports and Aboriginal cultural activities. Among the latter was Project Firewood/Rocks. With this project, SPS officers and Aboriginal youth went into the country to load a truck trailer with firewood and rocks to be used in sweat lodge ceremonies run by elders, some of which would be attended by the youth and the officers.

Playing the Starlight Tour Game: The Evan Maud Story

The story sounded eerily familiar. A young Aboriginal man claimed that two police officers in an unmarked car forced him inside their vehicle, took him outside of town, and dumped him there to walk back in the bitter cold of early prairie winter, December 3, 2010. There, so the story went, he was made to change out of his warm jacket and sweater and into a hoodie and then told to run home, or he would be shocked with a taser.

The teller of this story was 20-year-old Evan Maud. He became an instant celebrity when he lodged a complaint with the police on December 11. Academics and local media jumped onto the case, telling of how the Saskatoon phenomenon of 10 years before, the starlight tour was now taking place in Winnipeg.

The problem was the story was an almost complete fabrication. Yes, the officers had made contact with him, but it was to take him from out of the centre of traffic, for his own safety. They did check for prior offenses, and then left him where he was. There was video evidence of him entering a bus 15 minutes after the encounter. GPS data from the car showed that it never left the city. And there were also eye-witness accounts placing him in the bus.

The Assembly of Manitoba Chiefs was put into an awkward position. They served as liaison between Maud and the police and supported him, but Grand Chief Ron Evans expressed concern that the claims would damage the developing relationship between the WPS and the Aboriginal community. Once you feel you are part of the system, you have to be more careful who you offend.

Urban Reserves in Saskatoon

In the province of Saskatchewan a new type of small, urban, mini-reserve came into being in the late 1980s. These **urban reserves** as they are called came about as many of the treaty land entitlements in Saskatchewan–that is, the land promised the Aboriginal people of that province over 100 years ago–were yet to be given to the people to whom they are owed. Unfulfilled federal government treaty promises have long been a major grievance among Aboriginal people. As an increasing percentage of Aboriginal people in Saskatchewan are moving into urban areas such as Regina, Saskatoon, and Prince Albert, and as a good number of rural reserves have little solid economic foundation, it was thought that land should be purchased through the Saskatchewan Treaty Land Entitlement Framework Agreement (signed in 1992). Twenty-eight of the 70 Saskatchewan First Nations signed on.

The band that owns the reserve pays fee-for-service calculated in the same way that urban property taxes are figured out. These services include such key elements as policing, fire fighting, and garbage and snow removal, with electricity and water being paid for by individual Aboriginal business establishments.

There are currently three such urban reserves in Saskatoon. The earliest established and largest is owned by the Muskeg Lake Cree Nation, whose main reserve is located some 93 kilometres outside of Saskatoon. The urban reserve includes some 33 acres of land with businesses employing over 300 people. It is similar in nature to an urban industrial park. Almost all of the businesses are Aboriginal owned. Anyone can walk onto the land and do business.

The two other urban reserves are individual businesses. One is the Cree Way Gas West, run by the Muskeg Lake Cree Nation, and the other is the Fire Creek Gas and Grill, run by the One Arrow First Nation.

Conclusions

I have written in this chapter about a practice called starlight tours, practices that have led to the death of some Aboriginal males, particularly Neil Stonechild in 1990. The practice, and the inadequate way that it was dealt with by the police when it was a suspected cause in the death by hypothermia of Aboriginal men, stand as clear indicators of the unhealthy relationship between Aboriginal people and the Saskatoon Policing Service at that time and at the time of the inquiry that followed. This unhealthy relationship developed in the context of a relatively rapid migration of significant numbers of Aboriginal people into Saskatoon, with senior police administration and city facilities (e.g., a detox centre) not being prepared for such a situation.

Several strategies are required to heal this relationship. The SPS has taken some positive steps in this regard, including hiring more Aboriginal officers and getting involved with at-risk Aboriginal youth. What is further required, if it has not happened already, is for there to be an Aboriginal officer responsible for handling complaints about the police from Aboriginal people. This person should have both the respect of the local Aboriginal community and should have enough senior standing that police administration will have to listen to what he or she has to say. Complaints need not only to be taken seriously, but to be seen to be taken seriously.

Questions

1. What do you think the effects of the rapid growth in the Aboriginal population of Saskatoon were on how non-Aboriginal police have dealt with Aboriginal people?
2. If you were to design policing programs in Saskatoon that have as their main purpose greater communication and mutual respect between the Aboriginal population and the Saskatoon Police Service, how would information concerning all of these factors be best employed?
3. What challenges do these factors present to the Saskatoon Police Service?
4. Do you think that the officers convicted of unlawful confinement in the Darrell Night case were scapegoats for:
    a. other officers who may have been involved with the practice of starlight tours?
    b. the systemic racism involved with the justice system in Saskatoon?
5. Is it reasonable to link the deaths of Dustyhorn and Ironchild with those of Aboriginal men who were taken on starlight tours? Keep in mind that:
    a. if the men had been taken to detox centres or a hospital they probably would have survived;
    b. the police made sure that both men were given reliable transportation home.
6. Do you think that the percentage of Aboriginal police officers is high enough to significantly improve policing for Aboriginal people in Saskatoon?
7. Do you think that the under-representation among supervisors, executives, and civilians is significant in terms of the quality of policing dealing with Aboriginal people in Saskatoon?

8. Do you think that there should be in Saskatoon an Aboriginal detox centre with an entire staff of Aboriginal people? Do you think it would be more effective than what is in place now?

9. Do you think that the detox centre might be abused by as the police as a simple holding tank for "Indians," as the Main Street Project in Winnipeg has been?

10. Do you think that having a significant number of Aboriginal-run businesses in Saskatoon will improve the relationship between Aboriginal people and the SPS (at least by changing stereotypes)?

11. Do you anticipate any policing difficulties with having urban reserves in Saskatoon?

12. How do you think the Evan Maud case would affect mainstream perception of the Saskatoon cases?

13. Do you think that cases like this will continue to arise? Why (not)?

14. How might this case affect how police treat young Aboriginal men?

15. What do you think that Mike McLean means when he says that you can provide people with the tools of change, but a change of attitude from within is required?

16. McLean also states in his article that there was "an undeniable amount of politics involved" with his job. Do you think that the politics would be coming more from institutional racism or from resistance from Aboriginal organizations to link with the SPS?

17. Why do you think it took so long (11 years) for a status or Treaty Indian to occupy the position of Aboriginal liaison officer? What resistance would come from each side, Aboriginal and non-Aboriginal?

18. Do you believe that only an Aboriginal police officer should hold the position of ALO? Why (not)?

Key Terms

median–this is the middle number of a series of numbers (e.g., with 1, 2, 4, 7, 8, the number 4 is the median). It can be higher or lower than the average.

political correctness–generally well-intentioned, if sometimes misguided, attempts to limit speech and writing by censoring words, and to restrict practices that exhibit and promote racism, sexism, classism, ablism, and other forms of discrimination.

sentencing circles–Aboriginal tradition-based restorative justice practices in which offenders and community members, including victims and their families, elders, and other relevant people discuss how a convicted criminal should be sentenced.

starlight tour–the questionable practice of driving offenders, usually people who are drunk, to the outskirts of town, leaving them to find their way back to where they want to be.

urban reserves–in Saskatchewan, these are small pieces of land given to bands for the purposes of industrial malls or single businesses as part of what they are owed from unfulfilled treaty commitments.

References

Anderson, T. (2010). 2006 Aboriginal Population Profile for Saskatoon (Catalogue no. 89-638-XWE). Ottawa, ON: Statistics Canada. Retrieved from www.statcan.gc.ca/pub/89-638-x/2010003/article/11080-eng.htm

Comack, E. (2012). Starlight Tour. In *Racialized policing: Aboriginal People's encounters with the police* (pp. 115-151). Halifax: Fernwood Publishing.

Cummins, B.D., & Steckley, J.L. (2003). *Aboriginal policing: A Canadian perspective*. Toronto: Pearson Canada.

Frideres, J.S., & Gadacz, R.R. (2012). *Aboriginal Peoples in Canada* (7th ed.). Toronto: Pearson Canada.

Frideres, J.S., & Gadacz, R.R. (2012). *Aboriginal Peoples in Canada* (9th ed.). Toronto: Pearson Canada.

Thompson, B. (Producer), & Hubbard, T. (Writer/Director). (2004). *Two worlds colliding* (Documentary film). Canada: National Film Board of Canada. Retrieved from http://www.nfb.ca/film/two_worlds_colliding

IANE Inc (Inter-Provincial Association on Native Employment) (2012, March 24). Retrieved from http://www.ianeinc.ca/awards.html

Kossick, D. (2000). Institutionalized violence in Saskatoon. *Canadian Dimension*, July 1.

Latimer, J., & Foss, C. (2004). *A one-day snapshot of Aboriginal Youth in custody across Canada: Phase II*. Ottawa: Department of Justice Canada. Retrieved from http://www.justice.gc.ca/eng/pi/rs/rep-rap/2004/yj2-jj2/yj2.pdf

Loreto, F. (2007). *Two worlds colliding* (Review). *Canadian Review of Materials, 13*(13). Retrieved from http://umanitoba.ca/outreach/cm/vol13/no13/twoworlds.html

McLean, C. (2004, April 12). Rush to Judgment. *Western Standard*. Retrieved from http://www.westernstandard.ca

McLean, M. (2008). Job was all about building partnerships. *Eagle Feather News, 11*(8), 7.

McNairn, K. (2004). Retracing Rodney Naistus's footsteps up to the day he died. Injusticebusters. Retrieved from http://injusticebusters.org/04/Naistus_Rodney.shtml

Perrault, S. (2009). The incarceration of Aboriginal People in adult correctional services. *Juristat, 29*(3).

Perreaux, L. (2000, September 18). Officers admit 'mistake' leaving man in -22C. *National Post*, A14.

Reber, S., & Renaud, R. (2005). *Starlight tour: The last lonely night of Neil Stonechild*. Toronto, ON: Random House Canada.

Saskatoon Police Service. (2007) *Annual report*. Retrieved from http://police.saskatoon.sk.ca/pdf/annual_reports/2007_Annual_Report.pdf

Saskatoon Police Service. (n.d.). *Peacekeepers program*. http://www.city.saskatoon.sk.ca/police/programs/liaisons/index.asp

Sociology Department, University of Saskatchewan. (n.d.). *Aboriginal justice and criminology program*. Retrieved from http://www.arts.usask.ca/sociology/undergraduates/abjac.php

Stackhouse, J. (2001, November 3). Welcome to Harlem on the Prairies. *Globe and Mail*, F2-F4.

Steckley, J., & Cummins, B. (2008). *Full circle: Canada's First Nations* (2nd ed.). Toronto, ON: Pearson Canada.

Steckley, J., & Letts, G. (2010). *Elements of sociology: A critical Canadian introduction* (2nd ed.). Toronto, ON: Oxford University Press.

Zakreski, D. (2000, February 17). Police Chief under siege: Dave Scott reverses stance, calls for outside investigation. *Saskatoon Star Phoenix*.

Conclusion

In his report as commissioner of the inquiry concerning the death of Neil Stonechild in Saskatoon, David H. Wright wrote:

> As I reviewed the evidence in this Inquiry, I was reminded, again, and again of the chasm that separates Aboriginal and non-Aboriginal people in this city and province. Our two communities do not know each other and do not seem to want to. (2004, p. 209)

He could have been speaking of any combination of city and province in Canada, or any part of Canada.

In introducing her review of Elizabeth Comack's *Racialized Policing: Aboriginal People's Encounters with the Police*, which discusses at length the J.J. Harper, Neil Stonechild, and Matthew Dumas cases, Aboriginal writer Shari Narine (2012) remarked, "the most disturbing aspect of [this book]…is not the first-hand experiences it relates in the pages, but the stories it mirrors from today's headlines."

Bridging the Cultural Divide

There is a great cultural divide between Aboriginal culture and policing culture in Canada, which is part of an even bigger divide between Aboriginal and mainstream Canada. We can see something of the police and Aboriginal cultural divide even in small aspects, such as contrasting the mottos of the various policing services in Canada, as compared with Aboriginal words for "police officer." The RCMP's motto is "Maintiens le Droit" (roughly translated from medieval French as "keep the law"). The Toronto Police Service motto is "to serve and protect." The OPP vision statement is a simple, "Safe Community…A Secure Ontario." Aboriginals first perceived police officers as outsiders who acted upon Aboriginal people without their consent. In the Algonquian language family, a grouping that has speakers in all the provinces of Canada, typical terms for police officers are derived from verb roots meaning "to grab, seize, capture," giving words such as the Ojibwe *dkonwewnini*, "a man who seizes" (Rhodes, 1985, p. 115). The Peigan term *iyinnakiikoan* means essentially the same thing (Franz & Russell, 1995, p. 266).[1] In Iroquoian languages (Mohawk, Oneida, Onondaga, Cayuga, Seneca, and Tuscarora), spoken in Quebec and Ontario, the term for police officer is likewise derived from a verb meaning "to catch" (in Cayuga) (Froman et al., 2002, p. 238) or "to take hold of, catch up with, get fits, receive, arrest" (Michelson & Doxtator, 2002, pp. 814-815).

In the preceding chapters we looked at five case studies in which the Canadian justice system was decidedly "unjust" in its dealing with Aboriginal people. These cases are distinct in their own way, but are also similar to a significant extent. All of them exhibit **systemic racism**, with some personal racism thrown in. I believe that if meaningful measures are enacted to take much of the racism out of the system, then the personal racism will decrease measurably. If you ever doubted the presence of personal racism in Canada, all you have to do is read the anonymous e-mail responses to articles in Canadian newspapers that take a positive view of Idle No More or anything that does not clearly criticize Aboriginal people.

One common theme in the majority of the inquests, inquiries, and royal commissions spawned by these cases is that the system was definitely racist during the time in which the acts of injustice were practiced. It is like the situation with being an alcoholic. The first step to correcting the situation is admitting that there is a problem. These cases revealed problems at different times and places. But there are also next steps that need to be taken. The justice system must be dynamic and adaptive in order to meet the needs of society. A static justice system is one that is unjust.

The key here in simpler terms is that it is not the existence of "rotten apples" of personal racism that should be seen as the primary problem, although individuals and organizations do contribute to the injustices that Aboriginal people face in the Canadian justice system. It is much more the case that the whole Canadian justice orchard in which the apples were found, some rotten and some still fresh, as it existed in the 1970s and 1980s, gave off a distinct racist odour. The trees were not healthy. It is part of systemic racism to believe that racism is just an individual thing or a personality defect.

Part of what may be called the "belief system" of systemic racism is comprised of **stereotypes**. They enable people to think and act as if what they are doing is not racist but realistic. The stereotypes of the squaw and the drunken Indian are integral to the problem. They need to be counteracted by replacing them with an admittedly more complicated, more accurate, and useful depiction of Aboriginal women and of Aboriginal people in general. The system changes are not merely those of the justice system, but need to take place in the education system, in the classroom, and in the media.

The specific education that police officers receive on their path to a policing career is improving. I do not think that it is an exaggeration to say that post-secondary policing education is advancing more in the direction of understanding Aboriginal history and culture than the general post-secondary system is in Canada. I know that my Police Foundation students learn more about Aboriginal people than the vast majority of their college peers, and more than their brothers and sisters do who might be going to university. That's a big step in the right direction. But Aboriginal culture is a very long way from being adequately incorporated into the culture of post-secondary education in Canada, which is necessary for stereotypes to change. Part of being "an educated person" in Canada should be having significant understanding of Aboriginal culture and history in Canada. In Canadian colleges and universities there are relatively few courses in Aboriginal studies, and Aboriginal input into world and Canadian history, political science, philosophy, literature, and sociology[2] is very slight if present at all in post-secondary textbooks and course outlines.

The Classroom of Personal Experiences

Similar and often more subtle changes need to take place as well in the realm of the personal experiences of police officers who deal with Aboriginal people in their work primarily "on the streets." Their learning in what I would call the "classroom of personal experiences" has to change. Those experiences have to be with Aboriginal youth at-risk and not at-risk (although the risk for Aboriginal youth in spending jail time is much higher than other youth, even accounting for class status). Aboriginal urban communities themselves have some work to do as well. They are part of the justice system even if they do not make concrete initiatives to the force. We need to have more moves from both sides that work to break down the "we vs. they and they vs. we" dichotomy of Aboriginal people and police.

Although knowing and working with just one person who breaks a cultural or racial stereotype can bring about a great deal of learning, there needs to be an increase in Aboriginal police officers all the way up in the hierarchy for there to be a critical mass of those who understand the situation from the inside. Having a few scattered individuals, **tokens** that are Aboriginal is not the path to change and improvement. The culture of the police force needs to change.

The Matthew Dumas Case

This is a point well made by Elizabeth Comack in her detailed and balanced analysis of the Matthew Dumas case, the shooting and killing of the 18-year-old Aboriginal man that took place during the afternoon of January 31, 2005 in inner city Winnipeg. It has been compared to the J.J. Harper case. An individual was threatened by three Aboriginal males, reported aged 9-10, 15-16, and 25, with the suggestion that at least one of them was carrying a weapon. An officer surveying the area in his car observed Dumas looking suspiciously at the police car, appearing to be nervous. Officers who were involved on the scene reported that they did not understand why Dumas made the choices that he did: fleeing, resisting, generally not letting the officer see his innocence in the case. The judge at the inquest, Judge K.M. Curtis, even wrote: "Why he chose the path he did will remain an unanswered question" (Curtis, 2008, p. 66). They were essentially following the often-flawed there is no smoke without fire idea, which in this case meant "if he were innocent why did he act like he was guilty?" From an Aboriginal perspective, particularly an inner city Winnipeg Aboriginal perspective, one would very easily say: "Of course he acted suspiciously. He firmly believed, based on his prior experience, that as an Aboriginal person he would be considered guilty until proven innocent. Why would he think that he would be treated as a white person would?" I know that if I were an 18-year-old Aboriginal inner city Winnipeg youth, I would have acted like Dumas did at some stages. Part of having a policing culture that understands Aboriginal culture would involve some understanding of this. Imagine a world in which the police look at you as a suspect before they see you as a human. Here might be an opportunity for some kind of role-playing exercise.

The classroom of personal experience for Aboriginal youth needs to change as well. They need to see police officers in a variety of ways.

A related point made concerning understanding and changing policing culture relates to the flawed idea that "race was not involved" in the death of the Dumas because the shooter and another of the police officers involved were Métis. Here we return to the concept of **master status** discussed in Chapter One in the J.J. Harper case. We all carry various statuses with us (e.g., brother, sister, police officer, teacher, father, and mother). One tends to be the master status, the one that above all others defines who were are, what our identity is, and how people see us. In the Harper case, the important point was that, although his statuses included being middle class, a father, and other icons that people might respect, to the police officer that shot and killed him, his master status was "Indian." In the Matthew Dumas case, the master status of the two Métis officers is that they were police officers. In some senses, this is only natural. Police culture is strong; solidarity within the force is to be expected.

But in another sense it is wrong, and there is something that can and should be changed about it. What happened in this case, I would argue, is that the tragedy came about in part because Dumas was seen with the master status of "Indian" (and therefore suspicious), while the two officers (along with their colleagues) were acting solely as police officers, with predictable results.

It is difficult to be an Aboriginal police officer in the city. Here we can use the sociological concept of **role conflict**. **Statuses** and **roles** are different from each other. Statuses are positions that we hold and roles are sets of behaviours and attitudes that are expected to come with each status. When the roles that go with one status that you have conflict with the roles that go along with another of your statuses, then you are experiencing role conflict. If you have the statuses of mother and university or college student, and your son is sick but there is an important test coming up for one of your classes, you experience role conflict. You are expected, and you expect yourself, to take care of your son, but your teacher and you yourself expect you to study for your test.

If you are an Aboriginal police officer, you will experience role conflict when dealing with other Aboriginal people in the course of your duties. You can be accused (or you can accuse yourself) of being an "apple" (red on the outside, white on the inside) if you act only as a police officer. The same thing does not happen in the same way with white officers. If you are a white officer dealing with a potential suspect that is white, there should not be a role conflict (unless that person is a family member of yours, or a fellow officer that happens to be off duty). The status of Aboriginal police officer needs to be created, one that recognizes that there are different sets of expectations and that they both need to be responded to in some way. Individuals should not be left fight the battles of this role conflict on their own. This is just as important as having non-Aboriginal officers be trained to have greater understanding of what it is like to be an Aboriginal person. This is one change in policing culture that needs to take place.

The Sociological Imagination

A sociological concept to keep in mind is that of the **sociological imagination**. C. Wright Mills, a sociologist, coined the term and defines it as

> the capacity to shift from one perspective to another—
> from the political to the psychological; from examination of a single family to comparative assessment of the national budgets of the world…It is the capac-

ity of ranged from the most impersonal and remote transformations to the most intimate features of the human self–and to see the relationship between the two. (Mills, 1959, p. 4)

The problems that an individual police officer faces, Aboriginal or non-Aboriginal, when dealing with Aboriginal people, stem mainly not from the officer but from Canadian society in general. At the broadest level, the problem is not with police forces alone. To a significant extent, the weaknesses of the forces reflect the broader Canadian culture. Our education system does not do enough to teach Aboriginal history, culture, or its role in nature and the development in Canada (e.g., Aboriginal roles in our wars from the eighteenth to the twentieth century, and more recently in our fights to protect the environment). It has never been deemed important by those who develop courses and curriculum. It should be. Our mainstream media reflects and perpetuates this ignorance. To understand any "Native issue" from a balanced perspective, you must have access to Aboriginal media (e.g., *Windspeaker* and related news sources), not just mainstream sources. Aboriginal people have long been the "mysterious other," both romanticized "noble savage" and vilified "savage." Canadian police forces are parts and reflections of general Canadian culture. That, in large part, is the problem. Canadian society has long fostered systemic racism. Policing services are part of Canadian society.

Where Do We Get New Ideas for Aboriginal Policing?

We need new ideas to improve justice for Aboriginal people in Canada. One major source of new ideas is jurisdictions with similar circumstances. Look to other cultures. People who study **colonialism** will tell you that there is a great sameness of the colonial experience across the world. This is true. The way that Canadian governments, justice systems, and society in general treated Aboriginal people is not that different from experiences in other countries. **Paternalism** is a common feature. Outside of the obvious American examples, there are other jurisdictions that can help us a lot if we choose to study their experiences—where they went right and where they went wrong. The New Zealand experience can be very instructive. With them it was the British colonizing the Maori, and highly sophisticated Austronesian speaking people related to peoples in Hawaii, Samoa, and Taiwan. In a certain way, their experience is somewhat different. There is one major treaty, and all the peoples are closely related linguistically and culturally. The Maori traditionally had a more complex and sophisticated socio-political culture. But the basic colonial package was the same. Aboriginal people in Canada have over the last 20 to 30 years looked to the Maori experience themselves for new ideas, most prominently the Kohango reo or "language nests," which involve urban centres where elders are involved in teaching the language and culture to Maori children. Its success has led to similar developments in Hawaii and Australia. The Canadian government has not supported any such move in Canada.[3]

Of similar use is the Australian experience with the Aborigines. Again we have British people and laws and traditions imposed on an indigenous people. Like with the Maori, there is a lesser diversity in this area than among Aboriginal people of Canada, but the colonial experience produces similarity of problems and a hopeful similarity of potential solutions. Again, the beginning point is with a major government document, in this case the *Recognition of Aboriginal Customary Laws*, Australian Law Reform Commission (ALRC) Report 31, originally published in 1986, with updates online at www.alrc.gov.au. The key section of this documentary for our purposes is Part 32, "Aborigines and the Police." From their successes and failures we can learn.

I am an optimist. I work with both Aboriginal people and teach introductory sociology to Police Foundations students, and feel that positive change can and will take place.

Ten Key Concepts in this Book

1. Systemic or institutional racism is a much great cause of prejudice and discrimination than personal racism is.
2. Racialization affects all the component parts of the justice system, including a racialization of space, of the "usual suspects," and of witnesses.

3. The intersection of being both Aboriginal and female creates a multiplier effect in terms of the oppression and negative stereotyping affecting Aboriginal women.

4. A new respectful way has to be developed for handling missing and generally victimized Aboriginal women.

5. Policing culture has to become more influenced by Aboriginal culture (i.e., policing staff need to learn more about Aboriginal people and to learn to apply their perspective to a situation).

6. Aboriginal culture has to develop a positive space in which policing takes place.

7. The classroom of experience for policing staff has to be more balanced, with both positive and negative experiences with Aboriginal people.

8. The classroom of experience for Aboriginal people has to be more balanced, with both positive and negative experiences with police officers.

9. The stereotype of the drunk Indian is a major part of the difficulty police officers find in policing Aboriginal people.

10. The stereotype of the drunk Indian is a major part of the difficulty that Aboriginal people have with alcohol.

Eleven Key Books to Further your Knowledge

1. Cameron, S. (2010). *On the farm: Robert William Pickton and the tragic story of Vancouver's missing women.* Toronto, ON: Knopf Canada.

2. Comack, E. (2012). *Racialized policing: Aboriginal People's encounters with the police.* Halifax, NS: Fernwood Publishing.

3. Hamilton, A.C. (2001). *A feather not a gavel: Working towards Aboriginal justice.* Winnipeg: MB: Great Plains Publications.

4. Harris, M. (1986). *Justice denied: The law versus Donald Marshall.* Toronto, ON: Macmillan.

5. Kulchyski, P. (Ed.). (1994). *Unjust relations: Aboriginal rights in Canadian courts.* Toronto, ON: Oxford University Press.

6. Maracle, B. (1994). *Crazywater: Native voices on addiction and recovery.* Toronto, ON: Penguin Books.

7. McGillvray, A., & Comaskey, B. (1999). *Black eyes all of the time: Intimate violence, Aboriginal women, and the justice system.* Toronto, ON: University of Toronto Press.
8. Nihmey, J. (1998). *Fireworks and folly: How we killed Minnie Sutherland.* Ottawa, ON: Phillip Diamond Books.
9. Priest, L. (1989). *A conspiracy of silence.* Toronto, ON: McClelland & Stewart.
10. Reber, S., & Renaud, R. (2005). *Starlight tour: The last lonely night of Neil Stonechild.* Toronto, ON: Random House Canada.
11. Sinclair Jr., G. (1999). *Cowboys and Indians: The shooting of J.J. Harper.* Toronto, ON: McClelland & Stewart.

Questions

1. Why is the "rotten orchard" concept more meaningful in dealing with the key issues of Aboriginal policing than the idea of the "rotten apples"?
2. How does the idea of role conflict apply to Aboriginal police officers? How can that be changed?
3. Do you think that there is role conflict for non-Aboriginal police officers who are sympathetic to Aboriginal people? Explain.

Review of Key Terms

institutional or systemic racism–a situation in which policies, practices, and beliefs operate in organizations in such ways as to actively discriminate against one or more racialized groups.

intersecting oppression–the forms of oppression that occur when an individual possesses more than one negatively valued social status (e.g., race, gender, or class).

master status–the socially recognized position or condition (e.g., police chief, Aboriginal person, mother, disabled person, alcoholic, or queen) a person holds that is considered either by the individual and/or significant groups and/or society in general to be the one that primarily defines who that person is.

myth of biological helplessness–refers to the set of beliefs concerning Aboriginal inability to handle alcohol, to metabolize it, to drink and not act violently.

over-policing—refers to a situation in which the discretionary power of police officers is used consistently to over-charge or over-arrest or in other ways persecute a particular group.

panacea—an uncomplicated basic solution that is unrealistically believed to automatically resolve a broad set of problems.

paternalism—a way of treating people as if they were children, incapable of handling the basic responsibilities over their lives.

personal racism—a situation in which an individual's personal views and actions show clear prejudice and discrimination

racialized space—territory assumed to belong to a particular racialized group. This involves public space such as neighbourhoods, the "street," even being downtown at night.

role—the function assumed or the part played by a person in a particular social situation

role conflict—a situation that occurs when the roles that go with one status that an individual has is in conflict or competition with you have the roles that go along with another of statuses.

rotten apples—the idea that people do "bad things" (such as commit racism and sexism) because of their distinct personality, not because there is anything wrong with "the system."

rotten orchard—the idea that there is something wrong with the system, and this is why people do "bad things," such as act in racist or sexist ways.

squaw—the negative stereotype of Aboriginal women that portrays them as of little value except for their sexual exploitation and abuse by male oppressors, Aboriginal and non-Aboriginal.

status—a position held by an individual that is recognized by society as making demands on that person.

stereotype—an exaggerated but generally publicly accepted set of beliefs about a particular group, as if all members of the group participate equally in the (usually) negative aspects of the belief.

sociological imagination–the capacity to shift from the perspective of personal experience to the grander, societal scale that has caused or influenced that personal experience.

token–someone of an under-represented group who is placed in a highly visible position so that he or she gives the misleading appearance that an organization does not discriminate against that group.

Notes

[1] In Mi'kmaq, an Algonquian language, they use the more neutral *gast'pl,* derived from the word "constable" (http://www.mikmaqonline.org/).

[2] See Steckley (2003) for a study of the generally poor quality of Aboriginal issues in Canadian introductory sociology textbooks.

[3] Recommended reading of the Maori experience with policing in New Zealand is the *Report on Combating and Preventing Maori Crime* by Peter Doone (http://www.justice.govt.nz).

References

Curtis, K.M. (2008). *The Fatalities Inquiries Act.* Report by Provincial Judge on inquest respecting the death of Matthew Adam Joseph Dumas. Winnipeg: The Provincial Court of Manitoba. Retrieved from http://www.manitobacourts.mb.ca

Doone, P. (2000). *Report on combating and preventing Maori crime.* Retrieved from http://www.justice.govt.nz/publications-archived/2000

Franz, D.G., & Russell, N.J. (1995). *Blackfoot dictionary of stems, roots and affixes* (2nd ed.). Toronto, ON: University of Toronto Press.

Froman, F., Keye, A., Keye, L., & Dyck, C. (year). *English-Cayuga/Cayuga-English dictionary,* Toronto, ON: University of Toronto Press.

Michelson, K., & Doxtator, M. (2002). *Oneida-English/English-Oneida dictionary*, Toronto, ON: University of Toronto Press.

Mills, C. Wright. (1959). *The sociological imagination.* New York, NY: Oxford University Press.

Narine, S. (2012). *Widen the gaze beyond profiling and racism.* Retrieved from http://www.ammsa.com

Rhodes, R. (1985). *Eastern Ojibwa-Chippewa-Ottawa dictionary.* Amsterdam: Mouton Pub.

Steckley, J.L. (2003). *Aboriginal voices and the politics of representation in Canadian sociology textbooks.* Toronto, ON: Canadian Scholars Press.

Wright, D.H. (2004). *Report of the commission of inquiry relating to the death of Neil Stonechild.* Regina.

Index

Key Terms

CPSIA information can be obtained at www.ICGtesting.com
Printed in the USA
BVOW11s1726040915

416542BV00022B/359/P